READING

**A Workbook for the
Television Series**

Written By
Alan K. Garinger

The Kentucky
Network

The KET/GED Series is produced by KET, The Kentucky Network and Mississippi Educational Television.

ISBN 0-910475-30-X   2   3   4   5

KET Foundation, Inc.
600 Cooper Drive, Lexington, KY 40502

KET, The Kentucky Network
600 Cooper Drive, Lexington, KY 40502

READING

Contents

How To Use This Book

This workbook has one chapter for each of the video programs in the Reading Series. Each chapter of the workbook is divided into six parts. Look for boxes like these:

Preview of the Video	Goal-Setting Exercise	Viewing Prescription
Vocabulary	**Review**	**Practice**

First, Prepare for the Program ...

The first thing in the chapter is a **Preview of the Video**, which will tell you what the program and the chapter are about. Then there is a **Goal-Setting Exercise** to help you find out what parts of the program will help you the most. Complete the exercise and check your answers. Then read the **Viewing Prescription** to see which of the reading skills you should concentrate on. Finally, study the **Vocabulary**. These definitions will help you understand the material in the program.

... Then Watch ...

If you have read the preview, completed the exercises, and studied the Viewing Prescription and the vocabulary, you should really be primed for the program.

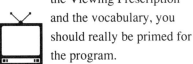

You'll see this symbol, which means it's time to watch the video program that goes with the

workbook chapter. Remember your personal Viewing Prescription and pay close attention to the things you had trouble with in the Goal-Setting Exercise. Listen for the vocabulary words; be sure you understand how they are used in the program.

... Then Review and Practice What You've Learned

Read over the **Subject Matter Review**, checking to be sure you noticed the important things in the video. Then practice the skills in the workbook with the reading selections.

If you think you need a little more practice before going on to the next chapter, complete the Extra Practice exercise at the end of the chapter.

This series will help you learn skills and subject matter. But each chapter in this workbook also contains a Test-Taking Tip—a hint or suggestion to help you when the time comes to test what you've learned.

Teacher's Introduction

These reading skills materials are designed to take advantage of the strengths of three media. Television is an incomparable motivator. The workbook has the advantage of immediate access and instant review. Computer software can individualize the instruction, quiz, and provide immediate reinforcement. These three media, when skillfully blended, produce a powerful learning opportunity for adult learners.

The Design

This is not a basic reading program. Rather, it is for students who already possess the basic skills and need to improve their interpretation skills.

The teaching scheme follows the classic formula: Introduce the skills and subject matter, then apply them in familiar situations.

This television series is unique in its treatment of the reading skills. The first five lessons introduce the skills by using literature and interpretation of visuals. These same reading skills are applied to science and social studies in the next 11 lessons. The science and social studies segments emphasize reading in these subjects and review major concepts in science and social studies.

About the Format

The lessons are arranged to encourage learner independence. The video program is previewed, a self-scoring Goal-Setting Exercise is completed, and vocabulary is introduced before the video is viewed.

The lessons provide practice through the use of multiple-choice questions similar to those on many standardized tests. The workbook also includes some short-answer responses. While these written exercises are important, it isn't necessary for them to be "graded."

Test-Taking Tips

The series will also help students become more test-wise. Each chapter has a test-taking suggestion, related to the subject matter of that lesson.

Extra Practice

These sections serve any of three purposes 1) reinforcement; 2) "fast tracking" for students with higher skill levels; and 3) quick review, after all lessons have been completed.

Pre-Test

DIRECTIONS: Circle the best answer for each question.

Questions 1-7 refer to the following passage.

Many people admire "idea people" as if they were geniuses and envy the flights of fancy these "thinkers" enjoy. Contrary to popular belief, however, idea generation is an affliction, a progressive disease, every bit as debilitating as alcoholism. Idea generation can be all-consuming, obsessive, even degrading. People tormented with this "talent" deserve our sympathy and help. Maybe someone should start an organization called "Ideas Anonymous." Hmmmm, that gives me an idea!

1. Which of the following tells what this passage is about?
   1) alcoholism
   2) ideas
   3) people who have ideas
   4) Ideas Anonymous
   5) how ideas work

2. Which of the following would be the best
   title for this passage?
   1) Ideas Are for the Birds
   2) As Bad as Lots of Other Things
   3) Just Another Obsession
   4) Pity the Poor Idea Person
   5) Be Careful What You Think

3. The word "debilitating" means
   1) disabling
   2) helpful
   3) interesting
   4) costly
   5) intoxicating

4. The author compares generating ideas with
   1) a talent
   2) flying
   3) alcoholism
   4) all of the above
   5) none of the above

5. The author wrote "talent" in quotes because
   1) it's grammatically correct
   2) it's spelled wrong
   3) someone said it
   4) he doesn't think it *is* a talent
   5) it looks better that way

6. The tone of this article makes you believe
   that the author
   1) is joking
   2) is dead serious
   3) thinks ideas are unimportant
   4) thinks people with ideas should be pitied
   5) is afraid he will get an idea

7. In the last line of the passage, the author
   says he has an idea. Which of the following
   best explains his idea?
   1) He's going to become an "idea person."
   2) He has an obsession.
   3) He plans to organize "Ideas Anonymous."
   4) There's no way to know.
   5) He's afraid to get an idea.

Read the following poem. Questions 8-11 refer to this poem.

Something sinister is in a cat
I'd call it love
Except
She caresses herself
Not me
Just against me
I'd stroke her head
But when I do
She hugs herself on my ankles
Making it hard for me
To walk

8. On the surface, this poem is about
   1) the way cats express affection
   2) how much the author doesn't like cats
   3) the way people share love with cats
   4) the sinister minds of cats
   5) 2) and 4)

9. Which of the following *might* the poem be
   about?
   1) war and peace
   2) animals don't understand human love
   3) a cat can get in your way
   4) how difficult it is to understand a cat
   5) self-serving love is troublesome

10. The author says the cat
    1) likes him
    2) isn't friendly
    3) is nice to be around
    4) is making love to herself
    5) none of the above

11. Why doesn't the author dare to be friendly
    with the cat?
    1) He doesn't like the cat.
    2) The cat doesn't really like him.
    3) It only makes the situation worse.
    4) The author is friendly to the cat.
    5) The author is afraid of the cat.

Questions 12-16 refer to the passage below.

Some uncanny ways of maintaining a strong "gene bank" exist in various wild species. Herding animals, for instance, use combat to drive out the weaker or younger males, forcing them to find mates somewhere else, if at all. In this way, the dangers involved in close inbreeding are prevented, and herds benefit from the "new blood."

Because many birds live in enormous flocks, avoiding inbreeding is more a matter of chance for them. The community must be very large to offer an opportunity for mating with others that are not closely related. To avoid inbreeding, the now extinct passenger pigeon needed a vast breeding population. When over-hunting reduced the flock to a point below this critical number, even though the number may have been in the millions, the species was doomed.

One of the more apparent examples of genetic precaution occurs in a variety of finch which lives on the Galapagos Islands. Males of the species have two distinct songs. A female will not mate with a male that sings the same song as her father.

12. This article is mainly about
    1) the way animals think
    2) reproductive practices that strengthen species
    3) planned parenthood in the animal kingdom
    4) weaknesses in the genes of animals
    5) deer and birds

13. The article suggests that
    1) close inbreeding is undesirable
    2) animals possess a moral code
    3) weaker animals always find a mate in another herd
    4) nature has all these intricacies worked out
    5) 2) and 3)

14. A human practice that parallels the behaviors discussed in this passage is
    1) divorce
    2) polyandry
    3) laws against marrying relatives
    4) religion
    5) dating

15. This article says that the passenger pigeon became extinct because of
    1) lack of sufficient mating opportunity
    2) over-hunting
    3) need for a large flock
    4) all of the above
    5) 2) and 3) but not 1)

16. Which of the following statements best describes the passage?
    1) The article reports scientific facts.
    2) It is unsupported and is just the author's opinion.
    3) There is little truth in the article.
    4) The examples chosen might prove a point, but other examples might not.
    5) Nature doesn't work this way.

Now read this passage. Questions 17-19 refer to this selection.

Imagine you are riding in the back of a pickup truck which is traveling thirty miles an hour. You mark the place where your feet are and then you jump straight up into the air. Where will you land? Will the truck move on without you, or will you come back down on the spot where you were standing?

During the time you are in the air, you are still traveling in the same direction at the same speed as the truck. Fortunately, you will land on the spot where you stood before you jumped. You will, that is, unless you jump so high that the air slows you down or the smart-aleck truck driver changes speed or direction.

17. Which of the following statements best explains the above passage?
    1) For every action, there is an equal and opposite reaction.
    2) No transfer of energy is 100% efficient.
    3) Water always seeks its own level.
    4) Things in motion tend to remain in motion.
    5) No two objects can occupy the same space at the same time.

18. If the principle referred to in the passage were not true, which of the following would be the most dangerous thing to do?
    1) frying an egg
    2) swimming in a lake
    3) listening to the radio
    4) painting your house with a roller
    5) flipping a coin while riding on a jet plane.

19. A bowling ball dropped off the back of the same moving truck rolls when it hits the pavement. Which of the following best describes what will happen?
    1) The truck will immediately leave the ball far behind.
    2) The ball will roll in the same direction as the truck, but will quickly slow down.
    3) The truck will rapidly speed up because it is no longer carrying the ball.
    4) The ball will roll in the opposite direction from the truck.
    5) The ball will hit the pavement at a spot directly below the point at which it was dropped.

Study the graphs below and answer the questions. Questions 20-23 refer to information in the graphs.

TOP 10 TV SHOWS IN 1950

1.	Texaco Star Theater	NBC	
2.	Fireside Theater	NBC	
3.	Philco TV Playhouse	NBC	
4.	Your Show of Shows	NBC	
5.	The Colgate Comedy Hour	NBC	
6.	Gillette Cavalcade of Sports	NBC	
7.	The Lone Ranger	ABC	
8.	Arthur Godfrey's Talent Scouts	CBS	
9.	Hopalong Cassidy	NBC	
10.	Mama	CBS	

Percent of Audience   0 10 20 30 40 50 60

TOP 10 TV SHOWS IN 1980

	Show	Network	
1.	Dallas	CBS	▓▓▓▓▓▓▓▓
2.	60 Minutes	CBS	▓▓▓▓▓▓▓
3.	Dukes of Hazzard	CBS	▓▓▓▓▓▓▓
4.	M*A*S*H	CBS	▓▓▓▓▓▓
5.	Love Boat	ABC	▓▓▓▓▓▓
6.	Private Benjamin	CBS	▓▓▓▓▓
7.	Jeffersons	CBS	▓▓▓▓▓
8.	Alice	CBS	▓▓▓▓▓
9.	Three's Company	ABC	▓▓▓▓
10.	House Calls	CBS	▓▓▓▓

Percent of Audience   0 10 20 30 40 50 60

20. The graphs show
    1) the percentage of the viewers who watched certain TV programs in 1950 and 1980
    2) the networks responsible for the 10 top programs in 1950 and 1980
    3) the names of the top 10 TV programs in 1950 and 1980
    4) the number of viewers of these 20 programs
    5) 1), 2), and 3), but not 4)

21. Which of the following is the closest estimate of the percentage of viewers of *The Lone Ranger*?
    1) 30%
    2) 41%
    3) 45%
    4) 48%
    5) 50%

22. Comparing 1950 to 1980, it could be said
    1) Fewer people watched TV in 1980 than in 1950.
    2) NBC had a greater number of shows in the top 10 in 1950 than in 1980.
    3) Shows written around a western theme were more popular in 1980 than in 1950.
    4) Viewers' tastes in TV were pretty much the same in these two years.
    5) There isn't enough information to answer this question.

23. *Mama*, the last of the 10 in 1950, scored a higher percentage of the viewing population than *Dallas*, the highest-ranking show in 1980. Which of the following explains this situation?
    1) Fewer people watched TV in 1980 than in 1950.
    2) *Dallas* wasn't as popular as *Mama*.
    3) Viewers had a much greater choice of programs in 1980, so the viewing interest was spread around more.
    4) During the three decades, more efficient ways of counting viewers were developed.
    5) The differences are insignificant between the two years.

24. Which of the following is the best title for this graph?
    1) Three Decades of Viewing Preference
    2) Comparing the Top 10 TV Programs of 1950 and 1980
    3) Television Viewing Statistics
    4) What People Like Then and Now
    5) Changing Taste in TV Viewing

Questions 25-28 refer to the following reading passage.

On Sunday, October 8, 1871, Mrs. O'Leary's fabled cow kicked over the lantern and started the world-famous Chicago fire, causing a loss of 300 lives and millions of dollars in property.

On that same night, 250 miles to the north, a far more devastating fire swept through the lumbering community of Peshtigo, Wisconsin, killing 1,500 people and turning 4 million acres of virgin timber to ashes. The heat from the fire was so intense that people exposed to it virtually exploded. In the panic, inhabitants running from the blaze burst into flame and became cinders, along with everything else that would burn.

Chicago was well equipped to handle its catastrophe and received the sympathy and aid of the world. Not so Peshtigo. Few people, even today, know of this tragedy.

Chicago was rebuilt, as was Peshtigo. The millions of acres of forest were not replanted, however, and the open fields were soon filled with dairy cattle. Today, license plates tell everyone that Wisconsin is the "Dairy State," not the "Lumber State."

25. This passage is mainly about
    1) the Chicago fire
    2) a comparison of the Chicago and Peshtigo
       fires
    3) the devastation of fire
    4) the dangers of lumbering
    5) dairy cattle in Wisconsin

26. The author uses the word "fabled" in refer-
    ring to Mrs. O'Leary's cow because
    1) the cow became very famous
    2) the cow started the Chicago fire
    3) it fits the tone of the rest of the pas-
       sage
    4) the author thinks the story of the cow is
       not true
    5) the cow actually started the Peshtigo
       fire

27. The author suggests that
    1) people all over the world helped Chicago
       because they knew about it
    2) Peshtigo didn't have the equipment or
       organization to successfully fight its
       fire
    3) the Peshtigo fire was much worse than the
       Chicago fire
    4) all of the above
    5) none of the above

28. The passage suggests that
    1) if the forests around Peshtigo had been
       replanted, Wisconsin might not have be-
       come the "Dairy State"
    2) the Peshtigo firefighters were incompe-
       tent
    3) the Peshtigo fire could have been pre-
       vented
    4) the Chicago fire could have been pre-
       vented
    5) both fires served a good purpose in the
       end

Questions 29-34 refer to the following selection.

It was in the middle of June of 1775 that 1,600 ill-clad and poorly equipped militiamen slipped onto the Charleston peninsula toward their objective at Bunker Hill. Their goal was to put pressure on the British fleet in the Boston harbor. They moved beyond their proposed position to a more forward, but less defensible location on Breed's Hill, where they set up fortifications.

Still suffering the embarrassment and losses of the encounter at Lexington and Concord, Britain's General Gage ordered his troops, under the leadership of General Howe, out of Boston to prevent the Colonists from shelling the harbor.

More than 2,000 British soldiers, well equipped and brightly uniformed, the best Europe had to offer, advanced shoulder-to-shoulder up Breed's Hill. At the perilously close range of 50 yards or less, the Colonists unleashed a murderous volley from their trenches and barricades, cutting the British ranks to pieces.

The British fled in disarray. They regrouped and tried again, and again the marksmanship of the rough frontiersmen cut them down.

Only after the British received reinforcements were they able to dislodge the rebels from the hill. The Colonists retreated to Bunker Hill, but then were forced to leave the peninsula.

It had been a costly battle for the British. They had sustained casualties to nearly half their forces. The colonists had "lost," but their heroism influenced many who had been reluctant to sign the Declaration of Independence. The battle demonstrated that there could be no peaceful solution.

29. Which of the following terms does the passage use to refer to the American forces?
   1) Colonists
   2) militiamen
   3) rebels
   4) frontiersmen
   5) all of the above

30. Which of these events occurred first?
   1) signing of the Declaration of Independence
   2) Battle of Bunker Hill
   3) Battle of Lexington and Concord
   4) British assault of the Charleston Peninsula
   5) Battle of Breed's Hill

31. Which of these events occurred last?
    1) signing of the Declaration of Independence
    2) Battle of Bunker Hill
    3) Battle of Lexington and Concord
    4) British assault of the Charleston Peninsula
    5) Battle of Breed's Hill

32. According to the passage
    1) General Gage sent only his best soldiers to Breed's Hill
    2) General Howe thought the battle would be easy
    3) the militiamen thought the battle would be easy
    4) Breed's Hill is north of Bunker Hill
    5) There isn't enough information given to be certain about any of the above.

33. The passage suggests that the outcome of the battle
    1) was discouraging to the Colonists
    2) demonstrated that the British were poor soldiers
    3) changed some people's minds about the Colonial cause
    4) was a decisive British victory
    5) proved that the Revolutionary War could be prevented by diplomacy

34. The passage emphasizes the
    1) difference in equipment and tactics of the two armies
    2) skill of the British generals
    3) quickness with which the British responded
    4) undisciplined nature of the Colonial army
    5) low morale of the British soldiers

Answers:
1. 3	2. 4	3. 1	4. 3	5. 4
6. 1	7. 3	8. 1	9. 5	10. 4
11. 3	12. 2	13. 1	14. 3	15. 5
16. 4	17. 4	18. 5	19. 2	20. 5
21. 2	22. 2	23. 3	24. 2	25. 2
26. 4	27. 4	28. 1	29. 5	30. 3
31. 1	32. 5	33. 3	34. 1	

CHECK YOUR
ANSWERS

These skills were tested for …	… in these questions …	1	2	3	4	5	6	7	8	9	10	11	12	13	14	15	16
Main Idea Directly Stated	1, 2, 8	✓	✓											✓			
Main Idea Indirectly Stated	3, 9, 12, 17, 24, 28	✓	✓			✓	✓		✓	✓	✓		✓				✓
Detail Directly Stated	15, 20, 21, 22			✓		✓	✓	✓		✓	✓	✓	✓		✓		
Context	3, 4, 5, 26	✓	✓	✓			✓		✓			✓	✓		✓	✓	✓
Fact or Opinion	16	✓		✓	✓								✓		✓		
Literal Language	1, 8	✓	✓														
Figurative Language	9, 29	✓	✓			✓	✓										
Inference	8, 10, 11, 13, 14, 19, 23, 26, 27, 33	✓	✓	✓	✓	✓	✓	✓	✓		✓	✓	✓	✓			✓
Compare/ Contrast	25, 34		✓	✓		✓	✓	✓						✓	✓	✓	
Cause/ Effect	28, 33													✓		✓	
Sequence	30, 31	✓															
Summarize	15	✓	✓			✓	✓	✓			✓	✓		✓	✓		✓
Motive	6, 7, 26			✓				✓									

Chapter One
Reading

You'll get a lot of enjoyment from this first television program, which introduces you to the Reading series.

Program One opens with a scene from the Edgar Allan Poe story "The Fall of the House of Usher." We'll use Poe's story to show you several ways to find the *real* meaning when you read.

This program demonstrates how you can figure out the definition of any unfamiliar word just by the way it fits into the words around it.

Sometimes we have to read between the lines to understand the full meaning of some types of writing. That's why this program discusses what figures of speech are all about. Incidentally, "read between the lines" is a figure of speech.

Goal-Setting Exercise for Program 1

Read this article and circle the correct answers to the questions.

> **During Colonial days, window glass was taxed by England. A few defiant Colonists started using the imperfect scrap ends of hand-blown glass for their windows. They did this to circumvent the law. Soon there was a great demand for the "Bullseye" glass, as it was called.**
>
> **Glassblowers found themselves intentionally making imperfect glass and more profit. They often "accidentally" broke the bubble of glass, leaving intact only the glass where it was connected to the blowpipe.**

1. Which of the following is the best title for this story?
   1) England Taxed the Colonies
   2) A Short History of Bullseye Glass
   3) There's Profit in Scrap
   4) Glassblowers in Colonial Times
   5) The Demand for the Bullseye

2. In this story, the word "accidentally" is in quotes because:
   1) someone said it
   2) it looks better that way
   3) it is spelled wrong
   4) the glass blowers probably broke the glass on purpose
   5) it's better grammar that way

3. You can tell from this article that the distinctive "bullseye" in the glass is produced by:
   1) a tax
   2) the way the glassblowers work
   3) the place the glass is connected to the blowpipe
   4) accident
   5) none of the above

Goal-Setting Exercise for Program 1 (continued)

4. The word "circumvent" as it is used in the article means:
   1) evade
   2) look around
   3) make glass
   4) obey
   5) follow

Answers:

1. 2   2. 4   3. 3   4. 1

CHECK YOUR
ANSWERS

Viewing Prescription for Program 1

Put a check mark by each statement that is an accurate assessment of how you did.

❏ If you got them all right …

marvelous! Enjoy the program, but complete the exercises in the workbook anyway.

❏ If you missed number **1** …

pay particular attention to the portion of the video that refers to understanding the *main idea*.

❏ If you missed number **2** …

understanding *figurative language* may be something you need to practice. You'll want to complete the Extra Practice at the end of this chapter.

❏ If you missed number **3** …

be alert to what is said in the video about reading for *detail*.

❏ If you missed number **4** …

be certain you understand how the program uses *context* clues. Many exercises in this workbook will help you with this important skill, too.

Vocabulary for Program 1

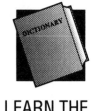

LEARN THE WORDS

context (KAHN-text) is used in this chapter to mean the way a word or phrase fits in with the words around it.

literal meaning (LIT-ur-ul) is a meaning that is exactly as stated. The literal meaning of the sentence "The king has fallen" is just that: You'd expect to see the king in a heap on the ground. (Compare with figurative meaning.)

figurative meaning (FIG-yur-uh-tiv) is the opposite of literal. A figurative translation of the sentence "The king has fallen" could be that he has lost his power.

metaphor (MET-uh-for) is a figurative comparison. It calls a person or an object something that it really isn't. (He *was* a real *mad bull*.)

simile (SIM-uh-lee) is a lot like a metaphor except it uses the words "like" or "as" in the comparison. (He behaved *like* a mad bull.)

inference (IN-fur-enss), in reading, is a conclusion you draw from what is read though it isn't directly stated.

abstract (AB-strakt) is something imaginary. You can't touch it. Ideas are abstract. So are love and the other emotions you feel.

concrete (kon-KREET) as used in this lesson means something you can touch. It is the opposite of "abstract."

idiom (ID-ee-uhm) is an expression that can't be interpreted word-for-word because the combination of words has a special meaning. "An idea out of the blue" is an example.

NOW
WATCH
PROGRAM
1

Several reading skills were covered in this program. Let's look at the important ones.

LEARN THE
SKILLS

Main Idea

Ask yourself, "What is the story all about? Is it stated directly, or do I have to look for clues that suggest the theme?" The program showed you that the main idea may be directly stated, it may appear in one sentence, or it may be scattered throughout the passage.

Being a good reader is a lot like being a good detective. You must constantly seek the clues that will help you understand what you read. Here are a few helpers.

Reading for the Main Idea

Below is a checklist to help you identify the main idea.

1) LOOK FOR A TOPIC SENTENCE.
Does one sentence say what the passage is about? If so, you've found the *topic* sentence.

2) LOOK WHERE IT'S LIKELY TO BE.
The topic sentence of a paragraph is likely to be at the beginning or close to the end of a paragraph. You can't count on it 100 percent of the time, but try looking in those places first. Here's one example:

> **Edgar Allan Poe wrote many stories and poems full of gloom and doom. His poem "The Raven" featured a big, black bird that visited the writer "Once upon a midnight dreary" and spoke only the word "Nevermore." Poe's story "The Tell-Tale Heart" is about a murderer who goes mad because he keeps hearing the beat of his victim's heart.**

The topic sentence is the first one in this paragraph. The other sentences contain details that support the main idea.

Find the main idea in this short passage:

> Pedro Serrano, Phillip Quarrll, Bruce Gordon, and Daniel Foss lived in four different centuries yet shared a rare experience. Like Robinson Crusoe, they were shipwrecked sailors who were marooned for a total of 71 years. All but one of them returned to civilization after being rescued.
>
> The one exception was Phillip Quarrll, who refused to return to his native England when finally discovered after living 50 years on a small Pacific island. The oddity of the Quarrll saga continues to this day because Quarrll's tiny island paradise was never included on modern maps. No one knows where the island is.

1. This passage is mainly about
   1) sailors
   2) castaways
   3) Pacific islands
   4) maps
   5) rescue

2. Which of the following would make the best title?
   1) Four Robinson Crusoes
   2) The Dangers of the Sea
   3) Pacific Paradise
   4) The Story of Phillip Quarrll
   5) The Adventures of Bruce Gordon

Answers:
1. 2—The others are mentioned, but the purpose of this article is to tell about marooned sailors.
2. 1—Calling these sailors "Robinson Crusoes" is a use of metaphor.

PRACTICE THE SKILLS

CHECK YOUR ANSWERS

Detail

The main idea doesn't stand alone. Writers use details to help make a clear picture in your mind. The topic sentence does not contain the entire meaning of a passage. If you think you've found the main idea, see if other information supports that idea.

LEARN THE SKILLS

Subject Matter Review (continued)

Read this paragraph and answer the questions.

> **Even a casual observer would recognize the dominance of cycles in nature. The water, or hydrologic, cycle, the nitrogen cycle, and the oxygen cycle are but a few examples. Even the seasons fit this pattern. So does life itself.**

PRACTICE THE SKILLS

```
1. What is the passage about?
   1)  life
   2)  the seasons
   3)  the dominance of cycles in nature
   4)  the hydrologic cycle
   5)  observation

2. Which of the following responses best sup-
   ports the theme of this passage?
   1)  the water cycle
   2)  the nitrogen cycle
   3)  the oxygen cycle
   4)  many cycles exist in nature
   5)  1) and 2) but not 3) or 4)
```

Answers:
 1. 3   2. 4

CHECK YOUR ANSWERS

Context Clues

To understand the meaning of a new word, it often helps to look at other words around it and try to guess what the unfamiliar word means. When you're trying to determine the meaning of an unfamiliar word or phrase, follow the suggestions below.

First try to substitute a word you know for the unknown word.

Example:

An ant carried a piece of bread with its <u>mandibles</u>.

What word will replace <u>mandibles</u> so the sentence still makes sense? If you can't think of one, select the best possibility from the list below.

legs, antennae, ears, abdomen, head, jaws, wheelbarrow

LEARN THE SKILLS

If the correct choice isn't obvious the first time through the list, reject the *least likely* and read the list again. (Odds are against <u>wheelbarrow</u> being right.) Did you pick <u>jaws</u>? That's the best one.

Sometimes an author will define something by comparing it to its opposite.

Example:

The timid opossum is totally unlike its cousin, the <u>sanguinary</u> Tasmanian Devil.

Let's see what you can discover about the word <u>sanguinary</u>. The meaning must be "totally unlike" timid. "Fierce" is unlike "timid," so that would give you an idea of what <u>sanguinary</u> means. Actually, it means "bloodthirsty," but "fierce" is close enough.

A related approach works well when you don't really need to *pronounce* un unknown word or term. Just call the mystery word "something," "someone," or "somewhere" and move on.

For example:

Some scientists believe that the mitochondria in our cells are evolutionary vestiges of primitive organisms which came to live in the cytoplasm of our cells and just stayed. A theory gaining favor in biological circles claims this situation is the very basis for symbiotic life.

Wow! That is certainly a threatening paragraph. Now read it this way:

Some scientists believe that the SOMETHING in our cells are SOME KIND OF organisms which came to live in the SOMETHING and just stayed. A theory gaining favor SOMEWHERE claims this situation is the very basis for SOME KIND OF life.

Reading it without all the words still leaves some meaning in the paragraph. The main thing is you got through it—you didn't throw up your hands in defeat. We loaded this paragraph with lots of unusual words. Most paragraphs won't have so many.

If you can't think of something that will replace the word, check to see whether the writer gave you a *second chance* to find out what the word means.

He stood in awe at the breathtaking sight of <u>Iguacu</u>, the world's largest waterfall.

If you didn't know what <u>Iguacu</u> was before, you do now because the writer told you. This approach works because when authors use words which might be unfamiliar to readers, they often define them in the same sentence. Words defined this way may be separated by commas, parentheses, dashes, asterisks, or footnotes.

<table>
<tr><td>

Subject Matter Review (continued)

</td></tr>
</table>

Figurative Language

When we use figurative language, we use figures of speech and express ideas indirectly. Understanding figurative language allows you to find the *meaning behind the meaning*. Figurative language expresses ideas about:

1. a character
2. a scene
3. a sensation
4. a situation

LEARN THE SKILLS

Which of the numbered items above best apply to the figurative expressions below?

He was a bear of a man.

1. What does this mean? _____
   _____
   _____

2. An expression of this type would be used mainly to describe:
   1) 2
   2) 1 and 4
   3) 1 but not 4
   4) 4 but not 1
   5) 2 and 3

PRACTICE THE SKILLS

Oaks stood like sentinels, guarding against the invasion of the night.

3. What does this mean? _____
   _____
   _____

4. An expression like this would be used mainly to describe:
   1) 2
   2) 1 and 4
   3) 4 but not 2
   4) 2 and 3
   5) 2 and 4

The fingers of death sponged the perspiration from my brow.

5. What does this mean? _____
   _____
   _____

Subject Matter Review (continued)

6. An expression of this type would be used mainly to describe:
   1) 1, 2, and 3
   2) 2, 3, and 4
   3) 2 and 3 but not 4
   4) 1 and 2 but not 3
   5) 1, 2, 3, and 4

Answers:
   1. The man had the characteristics of a bear.
   2. 3
   3. The trees reminded the author of soldiers.
   4. 5 is the best answer. 4 is OK, but not specific enough.
   5. It could mean that the speaker believes death is near.
   6. 5 is probably the best answer. The others might be right, depending on the context of the expression.

CHECK YOUR ANSWERS

Idioms

Idioms are a part of every language. They are sometimes difficult to understand because they don't translate word for word. An idiom is a group of words that is used to express a certain idea, even though each word alone usually has a very different meaning. Read this selection.

LEARN THE SKILLS

Think of an idiom as a secret code in the language. It is an "inside joke" intended to exclude those who don't understand the secret.

Idioms come in two general types. The most common ones make no sense at all if you translate them literally. "Raining cats and dogs" is an example of this type. The second variety says one thing but means something else. "Make hay while the sun shines" fits this pattern because it can be translated literally and figuratively.

Regions of a country develop their own idioms, which may not be understandable outside those geographic areas. How did the expression "Take an old cold tater and wait" ever get connected with "Have a little patience"?

Sometimes the term "idiom" refers to a specialized language known only to a select group of people. When it is used this way, it is usually preceded by the word "the." For example: "Sue will make a fine architect because she understands *the idiom* so well." This means that Sue knows all the esoteric architectural information.

**PRACTICE
THE SKILLS**

**Subject
Matter
Review
(continued)**

Now answer these questions. If you come across an idiom you don't understand, treat it as you would an unfamiliar word. Use context clues to help figure it out.

1. This article is mainly about
   1) idioms
   2) languages
   3) literal translation
   4) figurative translation
   5) different types and uses of idioms

2. "Esoteric" means
   1) architects
   2) foreign
   3) special
   4) faulty
   5) information

3. Three types of idiom were mentioned in the article:
   1. **No literal sense** (Ex: "raining cats and dogs")
   2. **Both literal and figurative** (Ex: "Make hay while the sun shines.")
   3. **Regional** (Ex: "Take an old cold tater and wait.")

   Categorize the idioms below by comparing them to the three types above. Write the number of the type in the space after each idiom.

   A. Y'all come back. _____
   B. cute as a button _____
   C. crazy like a fox _____
   D. I'm leavin' out._____
   E. Grits ain't groceries. _____
   F. Birds of a feather flock together._____
   G. Gag me with a spoon. _____

Answers:
1. 5—1 sounds OK, but it's too general.
2. 3   3A. 3   3B. 1   3C. 2
3D. 3   3E. 3   3F. 2   3G. 3

**CHECK YOUR
ANSWERS**

Read the selection below and answer the questions.

PRACTICE
THE SKILLS

The long-standing controversy over who actually discovered the North Pole came to light again as a result of a TV documentary which aired in December of 1983. The program asked whether Dr. Frederick Cook or Robert Peary first reached the Pole. Cook's trip was in 1908, Peary's in 1909.

The documentary, Race to the Pole, favored Cook and portrayed Peary as a tyrant and a fake. It told more about Cook's plight when he returned and the hatred the two explorers had for each other than about the actual agony of traveling the arctic north. The film stated that Cook had, indeed, reached the Pole first but Peary stole the honor through political means.

The National Geographic Society took the other side of the question in an editorial in the March, 1984 issue of *National Geographic* magazine. The Society's version accused Cook of being a fraud, not only in the polar expedition but in his other exploits as well. They went on to say that the documentary was a "blatant distortion of the historical record, vilifying an honest hero." The honest hero they were talking about was Robert E. Peary, whose expedition the Society sponsored three-quarters of a century before.

Whatever the truth may be, in 1911, the U.S. Congress offically recognized Peary as the discoverer.

Other explorers have entered the fray, too. Admiral Richard Byrd is said to have flown over the Pole in 1926. Because the instruments Byrd used to locate the Pole were far more sophisticated than those used in the days of Cook and Peary, some people believe he was more likely to have found the exact spot. Others still doubt his success.

The first man to set foot on the top of the world may have been a Russian with the German-sounding name of Otto Schmidt. His trip was in 1936, which makes the discovery fairly modern history.

The only bona fide, unchallenged conquest of the North Pole occurred in 1968, when four men, led by Ralph Plaisted, drove their snowmobiles across the pivot point of the world. Maybe, in time, this claim will be disputed also. Perhaps there are those who believe that the North Pole has not yet been discovered.

Now answer these questions.

1. The first paragraph is mainly about
   1) an argument over the discovery of the North Pole
   2) a TV show
   3) Frederick Cook
   4) Robert Peary
   5) Cook and Peary

2. The second paragraph is mainly about
   1) the North Pole
   2) Cook's political troubles
   3) the content of the documentary
   4) Cook's support for Peary
   5) none of the above

3. The third paragraph is mainly about
   1) Cook's claim to the discovery of the
      North Pole
   2) Peary's claim to the discovery of the
      North Pole
   3) a distortion of historical fact
   4) the true story of what happened
   5) the National Geographic Society's side of
      the story

4. Which of the following is the best title for
   this selection?
   1) An Old Controversy
   2) *National Geographic* Strikes Back
   3) Who Really Discovered the North Pole?
   4) A TV Documentary
   5) It Was Plaisted for Sure

5. Which of the following defines "blatant"?
   (third paragraph)
   1) careful
   2) unquestioned
   3) simple
   4) planned
   5) offensive

6. Which of the following best defines "fray"?
   (fifth paragraph)
   1) fringe
   2) discovery
   3) editorial
   4) dispute
   5) affair

7. Which word below best defines "bona fide"?
   (seventh paragraph)
   1) unchallenged
   2) fire
   3) discovery
   4) snowmobile
   5) false

8. Which of the following explains why *National Geographic* magazine came to Peary's defense?
   1) The Congress of the United States certified Peary as the actual discoverer.
   2) The Society was seeking the truth.
   3) The Society had sponsored the Peary expedition.
   4) Cook and Peary hated each other.
   5) Peary really did reach the Pole first.

9. Which of the following supports the idea that Byrd made the discovery?
   1) He flew over the Pole.
   2) He had better instruments than the earlier explorers had.
   3) It happened in 1926.
   4) He was an admiral.
   5) He was less controversial.

10. Which of the following does the article say is the only certain discoverer?
    1) Plaisted
    2) Peary
    3) Cook
    4) Schmidt
    5) Byrd

11. As the words below are used *in this selection*, mark them "A" for abstract or "C" for concrete.

    _____ hatred   _____ expedition
    _____ agony   _____ honest
    _____ film   _____ century
    _____ fraud   _____ instruments
    _____ history

12. Find two expressions in the article that refer to the North Pole but call it something else.
    1) _____
    2) _____

Subject Matter Review (continued)

13. List the names of the explorers in the order in which their attempts to reach the North Pole occurred.

    1) _____

    2) _____

    3) _____

    4) _____

    5) _____

Answers:

1. 1   2. 3   3. 5
4. 3—the entire article talks about the claims of several explorers.
5. 5   6. 4
7. 1—the article says "unchallenged," so, as far as the author's concerned, it's the best choice.
8. 3   9. 2
10. 1—the article says his conquest of the Pole is unchallenged.
11. A hatred   C expedition
    A agony   A honest
    C film   C century
    A fraud   C instruments
    A history
12. 1) top of the world
    2) pivot point
13. 1) Cook
    2) Peary
    3) Byrd
    4) Schmidt
    5) Plaisted

CHECK YOUR ANSWERS

Just For Fun

Limericks don't usually qualify as literature. Nevertheless, fill in the blanks in the limerick below. (*Hint:* In a limerick, lines 1, 2, and 5 rhyme and lines 3 and 4 rhyme.)

Said a struggling young writer named _____

When his bank account got very _____,

    "You just can't make _____

    Writing poetry, _____.

Even Edgar Allan was _____."

CHECK YOUR ANSWERS

Subject Matter Review (continued)

Answer:
Of course, there are many possible solutions. One solution is to fill in the blanks with the words <u>Joe</u>, <u>low</u>, <u>money</u>, <u>honey</u>, <u>po'</u>. This way, it is a play on words: <u>Poe</u> (Edgar Allan Poe) and <u>po'</u> (slang for poor) sound alike.

Test-Taking Tip

Many machine-graded tests are multiple choice. Below is an example of how such a question might look:

1. Which of the following animals is a reptile?
    1) robin
    2) elephant
    3) rattlesnake
    4) kangaroo
    5) earthworm

Your answers to these questions will be marked on a separate answer sheet. For each answer, mark your answer with a pencil as shown below.

The answer to the above question is "rattlesnake," so the answer space ③ is completely filled in. Since these answer sheets are electronically scored, don't make any unnecessary marks on them.

Chapter
Two
Reading

In this lesson, we begin to evaluate literature in different ways. The program starts with the poem "Mending Wall" by Robert Frost. Literally, the poem is about neighbors who are mending a stone fence. You will soon see, however, that the real meaning is much more than that.

When the program moves to a discussion of details, we see how writers use details to describe setting and characters. Then we draw some inferences based on details.

The final sequence uses an excerpt from Eudora Welty's story "Why I Live at the P.O." In this segment, you'll be asked to consider the emphasis a writer builds into the story.

Keep in mind the skills we talked about in the last chapter. Those simple techniques are the tools to unlock the "big meanings" mentioned so often in this program.

Goal-Setting Exercise for Program 2

Read the following selections and answer the questions.

Five-year-old Wilma sat on the back of the family dog, which was sleeping on the porch. Her brother, who was on a ladder painting the house, called the dog. Sport ran to Bruce, carrying a startled Wilma on his back.

1. This selection is mainly about   1. ① ② ③ ④ ⑤
   1) Wilma's dog
   2) what happened when Wilma sat on the dog
   3) Bruce's dog
   4) painting the house
   5) none of the above

2. Which of the following is the best descrip-   2. ① ② ③ ④ ⑤
   tion of the dog?
   1) It was large but friendly.
   2) It was large and fierce.
   3) It was small and friendly.
   4) It was small and fierce.
   5) There is no way to tell from the story.

3. Which statement below best describes the   3. ① ② ③ ④ ⑤
   children?
   1) Bruce was younger than Wilma.
   2) Wilma was younger than Bruce.
   3) The children were about the same age.
   4) Neither was surprised by what happened.
   5) They were afraid of the dog.

Goal-Setting Exercise for Program 2
(continued)

Read this poem by Emily Dickinson and answer the questions about it.

> There is no Frigate like a Book
> To take us Lands away
> Nor any Coursers like a Page
> Of prancing Poetry—
> This Traverse may the poorest take
> Without oppress of Toll—
> How frugal is the Chariot
> That bears the Human soul.

4. The author compares a book to a frigate. What's a frigate?
   1) a horse
   2) a ship
   3) a dream
   4) a courser
   5) a clock

   4. ① ② ③ ④ ⑤

5. Coursers are spirited horses. Which word in the poem helps us know that?
   1) Traverse
   2) Frigate
   3) Prancing
   4) Chariot
   5) Oppress

   5. ① ② ③ ④ ⑤

6. Which of the following best tells what this poem is about?
   1) reading books
   2) Ships are like books, people like horses.
   3) poor and frugal people
   4) chariots hauling human souls
   5) No matter who you are, you can have an adventure by reading.

   6. ① ② ③ ④ ⑤

Answers:

1. 2	2. 1	3. 2
4. 2	5. 3	6. 5

CHECK YOUR ANSWERS

Viewing Prescription for Program 2

☐ If you got them **all right** …   you're on your way. The video program talks about *emphasis*. Be sure you understand this discussion.

☐ If you missed number **1** or **6** …   you still need some help with finding the *main idea*. This program should help you.

☐ If you missed number **2** or **4** …   you didn't pick up the *details*. It would be a good idea to review the detail exercises in the last chapter before you watch the program.

☐ If you missed number **3** …   pay very close attention to what this program says about ideas that are *stated indirectly*.

Vocabulary for Program 2

interpretation (in-tur-pruh-TAY-shun) as it's used here means looking for clues that tell you more than just what the words say.

translation (tranz-LAY-shun) is related to interpretation. It implies, however, understanding such things as metaphors and figures of speech, which have meanings that are sometimes totally different from what the words say.

inference (IN-fur-enss), in this lesson, is used as a translation tool. Sentences "imply" a certain meaning. The idea you get is the inference.

conclusion (cuhn-CLEW-zhun) When you have made one or more inferences about an idea, the picture you get or the idea you end up with is the conclusion.

emphasis (EM-fuh-sis) is used in this lesson to mean the way a writer treats a character or an incident. It is a way of telling what the author thinks is important or unimportant.

LEARN THE WORDS

Subject
Matter
Review

Using details to help find the main idea when it is not directly stated is the most important part of this program. Let's look at some more examples.

Main Idea When It's Not Directly Stated

**LEARN THE
SKILLS**

The same thought process applies as it does when the main idea *is* directly stated.

Start by asking yourself these **key questions**: Who? What? Where? When? How? Why?

If the passage is to be translated literally, the exact answers to these questions will be in the story. Not every paragraph answers all the questions.

If the passage is to be translated figuratively, you must infer the answers to the same questions.

Here is another poem by Robert Frost. Read it and answer the questions.

**PRACTICE
THE SKILLS**

Stopping by a Woods on a Snowy Evening

Whose woods these are I think I know.
His house is in the village though;
He will not see me stopping here
To watch his woods fill up with snow.

My little horse must think it queer
To stop without a farmhouse near
Between the woods and frozen lake,
The darkest evening of the year.

He gives his harness bells a shake
To ask if there is some mistake.
The only other sound's the sweep
Of easy wind and downy flake.

The woods are lovely, dark and deep,
But I have promises to keep,
And miles to go before I sleep,
And miles to go before I sleep.

1. Which of the key questions are answered in   1. ① ② ③ ④ ⑤
   the first stanza?
   1) who, what, where
   2) why, when, how
   3) who, what, where, why
   4) who, how, why
   5) all of them

2. The main purpose of the second stanza is to   2. ① ② ③ ④ ⑤
   tell you
   1) who and where
   2) when and why
   3) where and when
   4) who and what
   5) all of the above

3. In stanza two, what is the date nearest the   3. ① ② ③ ④ ⑤
   time the story took place?
   1) March 1
   2) November 25
   3) January 10
   4) December 23
   5) There isn't enough information to know.

4. The third stanza mainly answers the question   4. ① ② ③ ④ ⑤
   1) who
   2) why
   3) where
   4) when
   5) how

5. If you translate the last stanza literally,   5. ① ② ③ ④ ⑤
   the narrator
   1) appreciates the beauty of the woods but
      must move on.
   2) is too busy to enjoy the woods.
   3) is sleepy.
   4) wants to keep his promises.
   5) wants to leave the woods.

6. Which of the following is the *best*
   figurative translation of the last stanza?
   1) If you spend too much time watching the
      woods, you won't get your work done.
   2) The narrator realizes he can't continue
      watching the woods forever.
   3) The narrator feels he has many things in
      his life to accomplish before he dies.
   4) The woods are beautiful.
   5) There isn't any figurative meaning.

6. ① ② ③ ④ ⑤

Answers:
1. 1—who (I), what (stopped), where (by a woods)
2. 5—who (horse and I), where (isolated woods), what (stopped), why (to watch the snow), when (darkest evening of the year)
3. 4—the darkest evening of the year
4. 2—the horse wonders
5. 1—2 is close, but lacks the tone of the passage
6. 3

**CHECK YOUR
ANSWERS**

When you are translating the "story behind the story," you are trying to get into the mind of the author. Many stories have several logical meanings. Part of the fascination in literature is that different people will get different meanings from the same story.

Details

Those key questions used to check out a main idea apply to some details, too. This is especially true if the detail is in the form of a figure of speech.

**LEARN THE
SKILLS**

Below are some isolated details. To which of the key questions does each one refer? Be careful.

1. "Beware the Ides of March"
2. under the tree
3. under the influence
4. as big as a barn
5. the parson's sister
6. the vinegar's mother
7. because she said so
8. around the clock
9. a near relative
10. beside himself

**PRACTICE
THE SKILLS**

Subject Matter Review (continued)

Answers:
1. when   2. where   3. how   4. how   5. who
6. what ("Mother" is a term for the white scum that sometimes develops on vinegar.)
7. why   8. when   9. who   10. how

Now read another bit of Eudora Welty's writing and answer the questions.

"Reach in my purse and git me a cigarette without no powder in it if you kin, Mrs. Fletcher, honey," said Leota to her ten o'clock shampoo-and-set customer. "I don't like no perfumed cigarettes."

Mrs. Fletcher gladly reached over to the lavender shelf under the lavender-framed mirror, shook a hair net loose from the clasp of the patent-leather bag, and slapped her hand down quickly on a powder puff which burst out when the purse was opened.

"Why, look at the peanuts, Leota!" said Mrs. Fletcher in her marvelling voice.

"Honey, them goobers has been in my purse a week if they's been in it a day. Mrs. Pike bought them peanuts."

"Who's Mrs. Pike?" asked Mrs. Fletcher, settling back. Hidden in this den of curling fluid and henna packs, separated by a lavender swing-door from the other customers, who were being gratified in other booths, she could give her curiosity its freedom. She looked expectantly at the black part in Leota's yellow curls as she bent to light the cigarette.

1. Which of the following best tells what is being emphasized in this passage?
   1) Mrs. Fletcher's hair
   2) Leota's purse
   3) the setting and characters
   4) the time of day
   5) lavender doors

1. ① ② ③ ④ ⑤

2. Where does the story take place?
   1) in Chicago
   2) in a beauty parlor
   3) Leota's home
   4) Mrs. Fletcher's home
   5) There's no way to tell.

2. ① ② ③ ④ ⑤

Subject
Matter
Review
(continued)

3. Which of the following best describes the   3. ① ② ③ ④ ⑤
   decor of the setting?
   1) fashionable
   2) artful
   3) bleak
   4) simple
   5) tasteless

4. Which of the following devices does Eudora   4. ① ② ③ ④ ⑤
   Welty use to describe the "feel" of the setting?
   1) repeated mention of colors
   2) use of dialect
   3) conversation
   4) descriptions of the surroundings
   5) all of the above

Answers:
1. 3   2. 2   3. 5   4. 5

CHECK YOUR
ANSWERS

PRACTICE
THE SKILLS

Use the same thought processes as you complete the exercises that follow.

Harry slammed down the hood, kicked the grill and started walking. It was the third time in as many weeks, but this time he was miles from civilization.

Two and one-half miles and forty-five minutes later, he was angrily shaking the door at an "all night service station." Right under the sign on the door that said, "Mechanic on Duty," this note was scrawled in felt pen, "We close at 11 PM on Monday."

The vandalized phone booth on the corner seemed like a solution, though forcing open the broken door proved more difficult than he would have imagined. The directory had been stolen. He inserted a quarter and dialed, "Directory Assistance." An electronic voice gave him Jim's number but failed to return his coin; his last coin.

He tried a collect call *without* a deposit. Finally a voice, not Jim's, but a voice came on the line.

"Tell Jim," Harry said, "I know where his Olds is. Have him call … just a minute …" Harry read the number on the phone in front of him. "Have him call, 555-7236."

If Jim had called back quickly or if the booth hadn't leaked when it started to rain, Harry might not have boarded the bus. He might not have risked giving the stern-faced driver a twenty-dollar bill for a 50¢ fare. He might not have been smiling as the bus pulled away just as the phone began to ring.

Now answer these questions.

1. In the first paragraph, what is happening?

2. In the second paragraph, when did this incident take place?

3. The next two paragraphs go together. How does Harry feel by this time?

4. Thinking of these same two paragraphs, which of the following would be the best title?
   1) A Telephone Call
   2) Harry Seeks a Solution
   3) Vandalism
   4) Long Distance Procedures
   5) A Lonely Road

   4. ① ② ③ ④ ⑤

5. Which of the following would be the best title for the last paragraph?
   1) Harry Has a Small Victory
   2) Harry Rides the Bus
   3) Bus Drivers Get Angry, Too
   4) A Rainy Night
   5) Vandalism

   5. ① ② ③ ④ ⑤

6. What is the *implied* main idea for the entire passage? Pick the one below that best fits your idea of what the selection is all about.
   1) a stalled car
   2) a long series of frustrations
   3) Jim's car
   4) vandalism
   5) Don't borrow a car from a friend.

   6. ① ② ③ ④ ⑤

Subject Matter Review (continued)

Answers:
1. Harry's car has stopped on a lonely road.
2. Monday, after 11 p.m.
3. He's angry!
4. 2
5. 1—Harry thinks Jim should suffer, too.
6. 2

CHECK YOUR ANSWERS

Now apply these same skills to this passage and answer the questions.

> **Wyoming biologists were concerned about the continuing decrease of trout in the state's streams. A century and a half of cattle grazing, mining, and oil prospecting had reduced most of the streams to sluggish muddy waterways unfit for the trout. Finally they found they could re-establish the beaver population and the animals would build ponds to settle out the particles in the run-off. The process of destruction could then be reversed.**

PRACTICE THE SKILLS

1. In this paragraph, does anything indicate that beavers lived in the streams before the trout died?

   _____

2. Does this paragraph imply any blame for the pollution of the streams?

   _____

3. Three polluting activities were mentioned. Can you infer which one came first? Which one?

   _____

Answers:
1. Yes—"Re-establish" implies the beavers were "established" before.
2. Yes—cattle raising, mining, oil prospecting
3. Because of the order in which the problems are mentioned, you can infer this is in sequence according to time.

CHECK YOUR ANSWERS

Skill Helper

REMEMBER THIS: The next time you're asked to find the main idea, pretend you have to send a telegram about the reading passage. It costs 50 cents for each word and you don't have much money.

**PRACTICE
THE SKILLS**

**Subject
Matter
Review
(continued)**

See whether you can determine what emotions the author is trying to convey.

"Richard Cory"
by Edwin Arlington Robinson

Whenever Richard Cory went downtown,
    We people on the pavement looked at him;
He was a gentleman from sole to crown,
    Clean favored, and imperially slim.

And he was always quietly arrayed,
    And he was always human when he talked;
But he fluttered pulses when he said,
    "Good morning," and he glittered when he walked.

And he was rich—yes, richer than a king,
    And admirably schooled in every grace:
In fine, we thought that he was everything
    To make us wish we were in his place.

So on we worked, and waited for the light,
    And went without meat, and cursed the bread;
And Richard Cory, one calm summer night,
    Went home and put a bullet through his head.

Now answer these questions:

1. Which of the following emotions did the   1. ① ② ③ ④ ⑤
   townspeople feel toward Richard Cory?
   1) indifference
   2) envy
   3) fear
   4) hatred
   5) none of the above

2. The townspeople thought Richard Cory was   2. ① ② ③ ④ ⑤
   1) a gentleman.
   2) self-assured.
   3) handsome.
   4) well dressed.
   5) all of the above

3. "In <u>fine</u>, we thought that he was everything …" Which word best replaces <u>fine</u> in the line above?
   1) case
   2) time
   3) fact
   4) order
   5) tune

3. ① ② ③ ④ ⑤

4. What do you think the townspeople felt when Richard Cory killed himself?
   1) shock
   2) sympathy
   3) indifference
   4) anger
   5) fear

4. ① ② ③ ④ ⑤

Answers:
 1. 2   2. 5   3. 3   4. 1

CHECK YOUR ANSWERS

Summarizing

When you **summarize** something, what you leave out is just as important as what you include. The omissions show that you have evaluated the situation and have determined that some facts are less important than others. Don't forget that sequence is part of summarizing.

LEARN THE SKILLS

In the space below, write a 10-line summary of your life.

My Vital Statistics

_____
_____
_____
_____
_____
_____
_____

PRACTICE THE SKILLS

Subject Matter Review (continued)

_____
_____
_____

Now write a main idea question, a detail question, and an emphasis question about your "vita."

_____
_____
_____
_____
_____
_____

Read this selection and answer the questions.

PRACTICE THE SKILLS

"A Devious Plot"

Important collegiate activities such as the "big game," fraternity hell week, and Friday's dance forced a certain college sophomore to high levels of creativity in his classwork for Beginning Composition 101. His finished product challenged the classic "Boy meets girl. Boy loses girl. Boy finds girl." as the record for terse statements about the plot.

He wrote the following "story" to satisfy his professor's assignment for a piece including _all_ these elements of plot: royalty, religion, sex, suspense, mystery, and humor.

**The princess screamed, "I think I'm pregnant!"**
**"Whodunit?" asked the priest.**

Now answer these questions:

1. Which of the assigned elements of plot *cannot be shown* in the article above?   1.① ② ③ ④ ⑤
   1) humor
   2) royalty
   3) mystery
   4) religion
   5) sex

Subject Matter Review (continued)

2. Which of the following phrases best replaces "for terse statements about plot"?   2. ① ② ③ ④ ⑤
   1) as the most complicated statement about plot
   2) as a short explanation of plot
   3) as a long, involved description of plot
   4) for timely ideas about plots
   5) for a meaningless example of plot

3. "Plot" means an outline of events in a story. Which of the following is *not* a plot? The story is about   3. ① ② ③ ④ ⑤
   1) a little girl whose pet sheep followed her to school and made all the other students laugh.
   2) the son and daughter of rival families who fall in love and cause much trouble for everyone.
   3) a private detective.
   4) an escaped slave who carries her baby across a river by jumping from one piece of floating ice to another.
   5) a man who takes his friend's place in prison and is mistakenly executed.

Answers:
1. 1—This is humorous only if you think it is.
2. 2
3. 3

CHECK YOUR ANSWERS

Just for Fun

PEDANTIC PARABLES. If "Refrain from investigating the dentition of a gratis equine" means "Never look a gift horse in the mouth," what do these mean?

1. An entrapped avarian specimen exceeds the value of a similar specimen residing in a bramble.

_____

Subject Matter Review (continued)

2. Though 103 are called, 10-3 are chosen.

_____

3. Monocots beyond the barrier are infinitely more lush.

_____

4. Lament not for lacteal losses.

_____

5. Seasoned observation provides a superlative pedagogue.

_____

Answers:
1. A bird in the hand is worth two in the bush.
2. Many are called, but few are chosen.
3. The grass is always greener on the other side of the fence.
4. Don't cry over spilled milk.
5. Experience is the best teacher.

CHECK YOUR ANSWERS

Parting Shot

The words <u>pedantic</u> and <u>pedagogue</u> come from the Latin word <u>paedagogus</u>. What does the Latin word <u>paedagogus</u> mean? <u>Pedantic</u>?

<u>Paedagogus</u> means "teacher." <u>Pedantic</u> means "like a teacher." This is not a flattering term, because it tends to mean "hifalutin'" (and that's a figure of speech).

Test-Taking Tip

Some standardized tests do not penalize you for guessing. We will say this again and again and even try to teach you some tactics that will increase your chances of guessing right. On these kinds of tests, it is important to answer as many questions as you can. _Rely on your common sense._

Of course, answer the easy questions first. There will be some that you're just going to have to guess.

In a question that gives five choices for the answer, you have a 20% chance of being right even if you make a wild guess. You have NO chance if you don't answer it at all.

Be sure to fill in the answer blank for every question.

Subject Matter Review
(continued)

Skills Checklist

❑ To answer questions that are about **inferred main idea**—Ask yourself, "Is there a bigger idea than the obvious story?"

❑ To answer questions about **details**—Ask yourself, "What smaller bits of information do I know which lead me to the main idea?"

❑ To answer questions in which **emphasis** is important—Ask yourself, "What does the author want me to think is important right now?"

❑ To **summarize a piece of writing**, ask yourself, "What are the most important things that happened and in what order? What can I leave out?"

❑ To **summarize a plot**, ask yourself, "What are the incidents that carry the story forward? In what order do they happen?"

Read the poem below and answer the questions.

EXTRA PRACTICE

Great Fleas

Great fleas have little fleas
   upon their backs to bite 'em
And little fleas have lesser fleas
   and so ad infinitum.
And the great fleas themselves, in turn,
   have greater fleas to go on;
While these have greater still, and greater
   still, and so on.

—by A. DeMorgan

1. Looking at this poem literally, it's about   1. ① ② ③ ④ ⑤
   1) fleas
   2) fleas
   3) fleas
   4) fleas
   5) all of the above

2. Looking at it figuratively, it's about   2. ① ② ③ ④ ⑤
   1) fleas
   2) imposition
   3) the end of time
   4) unanswerable questions
   5) all of the above

3. <u>Ad infinitum</u> means without end or limit.   3.① ② ③ ④ ⑤
   Which of the following is an example?
   1) words in the English language
   2) the people on Earth
   3) federal taxes
   4) the size of numbers
   5) the grains of sand on a beach

Read the selection below and answer the questions.

from
the lives and times of archy and mehitabel
by Don Marquis

Background:

According to the story, Don Marquis left a piece of paper in his typewriter overnight. In the morning, he found a strange message on the paper. It had been written by a cockroach named archy.

Archy typed by climbing up on the typewriter and diving headfirst onto the keys. Since making capitals requires striking two keys at the same time, archy could never do it.

expression is the need of my soul
i was once a vers libre bard*
but i died and my soul went into the body of a cockroach
it has given me a new outlook upon life
i see things from the underside now
thank you for the apple peelings in the wastepaper basket
but your paste is getting so stale i cant eat it
there is a cat here called mehitabel i wish you would have
removed she nearly ate me the other night why dont she
catch rats that is what she is supposed to be for
there is a rat here she should get without delay

most rats here are just rats
but this rat is like me he has a human soul in him
he used to be a poet himself
night after night i have written poetry for you
    on this typewriter
and this big brute of a rat who used to be a poet comes out of his
hole when it is done
and reads it and sniffs at it
he is jealous of my poetry
he used to make fun of it when we were both human
he was a punk poet himself
and after he has read it he sneers
and then he eats it

*<u>vers libre bard</u> means "a free verse poet"

Now answer these questions.

4. Do you *really* believe a cockroach wrote this?

_____

_____

_____

5. What is archy's point of view, literally
   speaking?

_____

_____

_____

6. Knowing that archy is a roach and knowing his
   point of view, what would you think the
   writings would be about?

_____

_____

_____

7. What is a major advantage of having such an
   unusual character as a cockroach tell your
   stories?

_____

_____

_____

8. Later in the story, archy says that mehitabel
   thinks she's "reincarnated" from an Egyptian
   princess, "probably cleopatra." How does this
   idea fit with the part of the story you just
   read?

_____

_____

_____

Answers:
1. 5—sorry! But a literal translation of this poem must mean that it's about fleas.
2. 2—Figuratively speaking, it isn't about fleas. That's what it's literally about.
   Therefore, the correct answer isn't 1. 4 is no good at all. A case could be made for
   3, but the most obvious answer is that it refers to the way imposition works.
   Imposition means to impose on or, in slang, to "bug" someone. See if this works.
   Everyone has someone who bugs him or her, but the "bugger" is also "bugged" by
   someone else. Got it? The interesting thing about figurative translation is that not
   everyone will translate it the same way. There are probably dozens of figurative
   stories this poem can tell.

CHECK YOUR
ANSWERS

3. 4—Numbers go on and on, but the others just seem to.

4. We don't know about you, but we believe it!

5. He says he sees things from the underside. This should give you a clue as to the kinds of things he would talk about. Marquis wrote several books in which archy appears with his other friends of the alleyways.

6. Archy always takes a point of view that is unusual. Add this to lowercase letters and you have the style of archy the cockroach.

7. The biggest advantage is that a cockroach can say something outrageous and get away with it. People often can't.

8. The passage you read talks about previous lives. It's natural for this theme to be repeated.

Chapter Three
Reading

Preview of the Video

This lesson could be considered a quick course in the tricks of the writing trade. If you understand the techniques of communication, you are better able to interpret what a particular story is about.

Mark Twain's *The Adventures of Huckleberry Finn* is more than just a story of a boy growing up on the Mississippi River. Its style alone tells us something important about what Samuel Clemens was trying to say.

Ishamel Reed then takes us to the movies. Unless you are familiar with Reed's work, you have never seen a horror show quite like this one. Or maybe *every* horror show is like this. Then again, maybe it isn't about horror movies at all.

Other selections in the program illustrate how critics use fact and opinion and how writers compare and contrast things. Finally, a scene from *Moby Dick* helps us understand cause and effect.

This program builds on the previous ones and challenges you to move to a higher plane of comprehension and appreciation.

Goal-Setting Exercise for Program 3

This program deals with analyzing what writers do to appeal to your senses. Here is a list of some of the writer's devices mentioned in this program.

<u>M</u>otives = the reasoning behind a statement or action
<u>A</u>ttitude = how a writer or character feels about something
<u>F</u>acts = things that can be tested and found to be true
<u>O</u>pinions = beliefs of the writer or of a character
<u>P</u>arody = a copy of a familiar literary form

Answer each question by writing the initial of the element it represents.

____ 1. Columbus was told that he would fall off the end of the world.

____ 2. *Where Two or Three are Gathered Together, Someone Spills the Milk* by Tom Mullen

____ 3. The shortest distance between two points is a straight line.

____ 4. "Shoot, if you must, this old gray head but spare your country's flag," she said. John G. Whittier, "Barbara Frietchie"

____ 5. "You won't find a better car for the price. Why, it was driven by a little old lady from Pasadena."

____ 6. A zookeeper didn't like the wildebeests. When they ran away, he said, "No gnus is good gnus."

____ 7. "A penny saved is a penny earned." B. Franklin

Answers for Goal-Setting Exercise:

1. O	2. P	3. F	4. M or A
5. M	6. P	7. A	

CHECK YOUR ANSWERS

Viewing Prescription for Program 3

❑ If you got them **all right** …   YOU'RE DOING GREAT! Enjoy the program.

❑ If you missed number **1** …   be sure you understand the difference between a *fact* and an *opinion*. The exercises in the workbook should help.

❑ If you missed number **2** or **6** …   study the definition of *parody* and see how the video deals with it.

❑ If you missed number **3** …   you may need to study the difference between a *fact* and an *opinion*.

❑ If you missed number **4** or **5** …   pay close attention to the discussion of *motives and attitudes* of authors and their characters.

❑ If you missed number **7** …   be sure you concentrate on the video and the exercises dealing with *attitude*.

Vocabulary for Program 3

satire (SAA-tire) is a style of writing that makes fun of something. It usually points to some human weakness.

dialect (DIE-uh-lect) refers to a particular style of speech used by certain people. Writers use dialect as a tool to develop characters.

parody (PAIR-uh-dee) is a story that copies a familiar style or form. Parodies often ridicule the original work.

LEARN THE WORDS

Preview of the Video

In this program, you saw how writers use characters, dialect, parodies, and attitudes to create images in the minds of their readers.

This excerpt from Jim Blaine's "My Grandfather's Old Ram," by Mark Twain, lends itself to a review of many of these elements. Read it and answer the questions.

PRACTICE
THE SKILLS

> **Every now and then, in these days, the boys used to tell me I ought to get one Jim Blaine to tell me the stirring story of his grandfather's old ram.... They kept this up until my curiosity was on the rack to hear the story. I got to haunting Blaine; but it was of no use.... At last, one evening I hurried to his cabin.... As I entered, he was sitting upon an empty powder-keg, with a clay pipe in one hand and the other raised to command silence. His face was round, red, and very serious; his throat was bare and his hair tumbled; in general appearance and costume he was a stalwart miner of the period....**

THE STORY OF THE OLD RAM

> **I found a seat at once, and Blaine said:**
>
> I don't reckon them times will ever come again. There never was a more bullier old ram than what he was. Grandfather fetched him from Illinois — got him of a man by the name of Yates — Bill Yates — maybe you might have heard of him; his father was a deacon — Baptist — and he was a rustler, too; a man had to get up ruther early to get the start of old Thankful Yates; it was him that put the Greens up to jining teams with my grandfather when he moved west. Seth Green was prob'ly the pick of the flock; he married a Wilkerson — Sara Wilkerson — good cretur, she was — one of the likeliest heifers that was ever raised in old Stoddard, everybody said that knowed her. She could heft a bar'l of flour as easy as I can flirt a flapjack. And spin? Don't mention it! Independent? Humph! When Sile Hawkins come a browsing around her, she let him know that for all his tin he couldn't trot in harness alongside of her. You see, Sile Hawkins was — no, it warn't Sile Hawkins after all — it was a galoot by the name of Filkins — I disremember his first name ..."
>
> [*Jim Blaine's tale continues, with much more of his illuminating detail. At the end of it, Twain writes:*]
>
> ... and the mention of the ram in the first sentence was as far as

**any man had ever heard him get, concerning it.... What the thing
was that happened to him and his grandfather's old ram is a dark
mystery to this day, for nobody has ever yet found out.**

Now answer these questions.

1. Which of the following best tells what Mark
   Twain's story is supposed to be about?
   1) Jim Blaine
   2) Jim's grandfather
   3) Jim's grandfather's ram
   4) Bill Yates
   5) Seth Green

1. ① ② ③ ④ ⑤

2. Which of the following best tells what
   Twain's story *is* about?
   1) Jim's grandfather
   2) Jim's grandfather's ram
   3) the family history of the Yates
   4) the way some people tell unorganized sto-
      ries
   5) picturesque speech

2. ① ② ③ ④ ⑤

3. Assuming Jim Blaine's tale is about the ram,
   which of the following best describes the
   supporting details?
   1) They are all directly stated.
   2) They must be inferred.
   3) There are very few.
   4) You must be kidding.
   5) Bill Yates's father was a Baptist.

3. ① ② ③ ④ ⑤

4. The editorial comment uses the term "illuminating detail." Which of the following tells
   best why this term is used?
   1) It's making a joke of Jim Blaine's story-
      telling ability.
   2) It describes a well thought-out story.
   3) The story *was* enlightening.
   4) "Illuminating" is the best word to de-
      scribe it.
   5) none of the above

4. ① ② ③ ④ ⑤

5. "Irrelevant" means not belonging or inappropriate. All of the following details are irrelevant to the story of Jim's grandfather's ram except
   1) his grandfather brought the ram home from Illinois.
   2) Bill Yates was a Baptist.
   3) Seth Green married a Wilkerson.
   4) Filkins was a galoot.
   5) Sarah Wilkerson was independent.

5. ① ② ③ ④ ⑤

6. Which of the following tells about Jim's grandfather's character?
   1) precise
   2) disorganized
   3) forgetful
   4) a sheep farmer
   5) You don't really know much about him.

6. ① ② ③ ④ ⑤

7. Who is the main character in Twain's story?
   1) the ram
   2) Jim's grandfather
   3) Jim Blaine
   4) Bill Yates
   5) Filkins

7. ① ② ③ ④ ⑤

Answers:
1. 3   2. 4   3. 3 is the best answer; 4 isn't bad.
4. 1—This is a form of satire.
5. 1   6. 5   7. 3

CHECK YOUR
ANSWERS

Because of the way our language works, certain signal words, or flags, indicate relationships between ideas or groups of words. For example:

Language Flags

Cause and Effect

They enlarged the grain bin <u>in order to</u> take care of the bumper crop.

<u>In order to</u> is a flag that indicates a CAUSE AND EFFECT relationship. The "bumper crop" was the CAUSE; enlarging the bin was the EFFECT.

Fill in the blanks with the best choice from among the words in the box.

FLAGS
for this reason
in order to
because of
it follows that
because
hence
since
therefore

1. _____ the Smiths were expecting triplets, they were going to need an addition to their house.

2. _____ high interest rates, Mr. and Mrs. Smith shopped around for the best deal.

3. _____ they were pleased, therefore, when the bank granted their loan.

Compare and Contrast

Fill in the blanks with the best choice from among the words in the box.

FLAGS
right
although
but
despite
even though
however
nevertheless

1. _____ his lowly beginnings, Lincoln attained his nation's highest office.

2. _____ in his life began in backwoods America, he learned to enjoy the glamor of Washington, D.C.

3. _____ he grew up in poverty, he later associated with the wealthiest people in the world.

Notice how each sentence compares one situation with another. Number 1—from "lowly beginnings" to "highest office."

Sequence

The flags below show sequence (order). Write your own sentence with each one.

FLAGS	
at that time	_____
in the meantime	_____
at last	_____
afterwards	_____
already	_____
during	_____
immediately	_____
while	_____
	_____

Summary

Writers often use the following flags to indicate a summary. Write your own sentence with each one.

FLAGS	
as well as	_____
the following	_____
another	_____
besides	_____
finally	_____
first	_____
furthermore	_____
next	_____
then	_____

Watch for these flags as you read.

Haiku poetry is a Japanese art form based on the number of syllables in the words. Each haiku contains 17 syllables, arranged in lines of five, seven, and five. Here's an example:

PRACTICE THE SKILLS

> **When my canary**
> **flew away, that was the end**
> **of spring in my house.**
>
> — **Shiki**

Notice that it tells a very simple, yet emotional story. Compare this next one.

**You can't ask a man
to tell you much more than this
in just a few words.**
— Jefferson Danyal

Now answer some questions about these two haikus.

1. In what ways are these two poems similar?
    Different?

    _____

    _____

    _____

2. Which of the following best tells what the   2.① ② ③ ④ ⑤
    first haiku is about?
    1) a canary
    2) spring
    3) sadness
    4) happiness
    5) the way houses are

3. Which of the following best tells what the   3.① ② ③ ④ ⑤
    second poem is all about?
    1) Saying something meaningful with a few
        words is difficult.
    2) It's just a parody to make fun of haiku.
    3) Only a few poets write haiku.
    4) Only poets who are not "wordy" would
        write haiku.
    5) There isn't enough information to know
        for sure.

Answers:
1. They are similar because they both fit the haiku pattern of syllables, and each one
    refers to one small idea. They are different because the first one is traditional and
    the second one isn't. Most haikus deal with nature or small bits of life. Only the
    first one does that.
2. 3
3. 1

CHECK YOUR
ANSWERS

Subject Matter Review (continued)

Tone

Part of style is tone. Tone tells the attitude and the "feel" of the passage or the characters.

Read the following selection and answer the questions.

PRACTICE THE SKILLS

> **Thomas Edison tested thousands of materials before he found a reliable one to serve as the filament for the electric light bulb.**
> **When asked if he was discouraged, he replied, "Certainly not! Each time I find something that won't work, I'm closer to something that will."**

1. Which word describes Edison's attitude about the experiments?
   1) discouragement
   2) tiredness
   3) confidence
   4) hopelessness
   5) exhilaration

1. ① ② ③ ④ ⑤

2. Which of the following best describes Edison's attitude?
   1) Edison worked hard to find something useful that would work.
   2) He was unsuccessful in finding the correct material.
   3) "Somewhere there is something that will work. I just have to find it."
   4) Science is discouraging business.
   5) He had to succeed because the world needed the invention.

2. ① ② ③ ④ ⑤

3. Which of the following conclusions can you draw from this situation?
   1) It was Edison's opinion that there was a material that would work.
   2) It was a fact that such a material existed.
   3) Edison's opinion proved to be fact.
   4) Edison's opinion was wrong.
   5) None of the above is a logical conclusion.

3. ① ② ③ ④ ⑤

Answers:
1. 3
2. 3
3. 1—2 seems right, but only because Edison found the material that made it a fact. 3 and 4 aren't specific enough.

CHECK YOUR ANSWERS

Fact or Opinion/Reality or Fantasy

The above exercise brings up the question: "Can an opinion be wrong?" If you say, "I think Emmylou Harris is a better singer than Jennifer Warnes," that *is* your opinion and it's hard to prove wrong. But to say, "In my opinion, a dozen is more than one hundred," shows an ignorance of the facts. This kind of "opinion" certainly can be wrong, because there is concrete proof that such an opinion is in error. Facts often can be measured in some way. Also, facts can be used to support an opinion. Lack of support can reveal that what we believe to be fact is actually opinion. Example:

LEARN THE SKILLS

1. Which of the following was the best baseball player of all time?
   1) Babe Ruth
   2) Henry Aaron
   3) Ty Cobb
   4) Joe DiMaggio

1. ① ② ③ ④ ⑤

2. Which of the following ballplayers hit the most career home runs?
   1) Babe Ruth
   2) Henry Aaron
   3) Ty Cobb
   4) Joe DiMaggio

2. ① ● ③ ④ ⑤

The answer to number 1 can be any one of them; this is strictly a matter of opinion. Your choice *is your choice*. The answer to number 2 is ②. It's a matter of record.

Read the selection below and answer the questions.

One of the worst floods in California history occurred between December 30, 1925 and January 27, 1926. During this month, 44 inches of rain fell, washing out 112 bridges. Many highways were flooded. Hundreds of boats were carried out to sea.

The Sweetwater Dam collapsed under the deluge. One day later, the Lower Otay Dam broke, sending a 50-foot wall of water down the canyon and drowning at least 20 people.

PRACTICE THE SKILLS

Subject Matter Review (continued)

All communications and power lines were destroyed. The floods cut off San Diego's water supply. The citizens were forced to find waterholes, which they shared with homeless wild animals, including hundreds of snakes.

First let's consider the facts. In straight reporting, there is little difference between facts and details. Make a list of the details in this article. We will evaluate them after you read the second part of this exercise.

FACTS:

_____

_____

_____

_____

_____

Now read the second part. This time we'll give you a different set of "facts."

On December 13, 1915, Charles Mallory Hatfield was negotiating a rather unusual deal with the city council of San Diego, California. Hatfield was a rainmaker. He promised to fill the city's drought-shrunken reservoirs by the end of 1916 or the council didn't have to pay him.

Hatfield and his brother set to work. By the end of the last day of December, they had produced just over an inch of rain. Not satisfied, they made their "Moisture Acceleration" formula stronger and tried again.

By January 14, their efforts began to pay off. On that day alone, it rained 4.23 inches. By the 17th, their "storm" had delivered almost 13 inches. The rain kept coming and totaled 44 inches by the end of the month.

Ironically, they were never paid for the job. Because of the destruction caused by the flooding, the City Council would pay them only if they agreed to cover the 3.5 million dollars in damage suits filed against the city. The rainmakers refused.

Because the brothers were afraid the information might be misused, they never told anyone their secret formula. It was lost when the Hatfields died.

Now respond to these questions and explain your answers.

1. Was the California flood caused by the rain-makers?

   ❏ yes ❏ no

   _____

Subject
Matter
Review
(continued)

2. Was the city justified in asking the
   Hatfields to pay the damages caused by the
   flood?
   ❑ yes   ❑ no

   _____

3. Is there proof in the article that the
   Hatfields were responsible for the storms?
   ❑ yes   ❑ no

   _____

4. Does the author of the second part believe
   the Hatfields were responsible?
   ❑ yes   ❑ no

   _____

Answers:

FACTS: a) California had a flood. b) It happened between December 30, 1915 and
January 27, 1916. c) 44 inches of rain fell during this period. d) 112 bridges were washed
out. e) Two dams collapsed. f) 20 people died. g) Communication lines were destroyed.
h) People and animals had to share the same water sources.

SECOND PART: The answers to question 1-4 are based on your opinion. The tone of the
article makes you feel the author believes the Hatfields were responsible.

CHECK YOUR
ANSWERS

Just for Fun

Writer Edward Stratemeyer created the heroic character Tom Swift, who
traveled from one adventure to another in his marvelous "electric aeroplane."

Stratemeyer didn't let his character just say something. He had to tell *how* he
said it—every time he spoke. As a result, Tom said things proudly, quickly,
happily, etc. There is no end to the *way* Tom could say something. ("I'll take
care of this situation," said Tom bravely.)

"Tom Swifties," puns that satirize this style, regain popularity from time to
time. Anyone can invent them:

"I just struck oil," said Tom crudely.
"Put down that razor," said Tom sharply.
"I washed the windows today," said Tom transparently.

Below are some "said Tom"s. Build speeches that fit them.

1. "_____," said Tom

   brightly.

2. "_____," said Tom

   woodenly.

3. "_____," said Tom color-

   fully.

4. "_____," said Tom dryly.

5. "_____," said Tom pride-

   fully.

Now tell *how* Tom said the things below.

1. "I certainly like this pineapple," said Tom

   _____.

2. "Observe the worm on this mulberry leaf,"

   said Tom _____.

3. "I'd like some ale," said Tom

   _____.

4. "That was a very loud noise," said Tom

   _____.

**Subject
Matter
Review**
(continued)

**CHECK YOUR
ANSWERS**

Answers:

The answers to the "Tom Swifties" depend on your imagination. Here are a couple of possibilities for each one.

1. a) "That was quite a bolt of lightning,"
   b) "This fire is so cozy,"
2. a) "I feel like a ventriloquist's dummy,"
   b) "Cut down that tree,"
3. a) "Come look at the rainbow,"
   b) "I spilled a gallon of paint on my head,"
4. a) "Here we are in the middle of the Sahara,"
   b) "I just ate a box of crackers,"
5. a) "There isn't room in here for this family of lions,"
   b) "Lou Gehrig played for the Yankees,"
6. a) dolefully   b) sweetly
7. a) silkily   b) scientifically
8. a) stoutly   b) lightly
9. a) explosively   b) deafeningly

Test-Taking Tip

When answering questions on a standardized test, the right answer is supposed to make all the others wrong. If you are in doubt about your answer, check whether your choice makes the others wrong. For example, look at these answers:

1) **The Confederacy**
2) **Southern Forces**
3) **General Lee's Army**
4) **The Rebel Army**
5) **Union Forces**

Without even seeing the question, it is obvious that answer 5 makes all the others wrong. Answers 1, 2, 3, and 4 don't do that.

Skills Checklist

In the space below, summarize this lesson. Try to remember skills mentioned in the video and also in the workbook. Be careful to place the important events in sequence, either as they happened or as you rate their importance.

_____
_____
_____
_____
_____
_____
_____
_____
_____

Each quote in one list has a mate in the other list. They should match on the basis of motive, dialect, cause and effect, characterization, parody, and fact or opinion.

**EXTRA
PRACTICE**

List I

____ 1. "Abandon your animosities and make your sons Americans." —Robert E. Lee

____ 2. "Theodore Roosevelt: Haranque-outang." —Roycroft Dictionary

____ 3. "The hurrier I go, the behinder I get." —Pennsylvania Dutch adage

____ 4. "I never saw a vitamin. I never hope to see one. But I can tell you here and now I'd rather see than B1." —unknown

____ 5. "For want of a nail the shoe was lost. For want of a shoe the horse was lost. For want of a horse the rider was lost. For want of a rider the battle was lost. For want of a battle the kingdom was lost. And all for the want of a horseshoe nail." —Ben Franklin, *Poor Richard's Almanac*

____ 6. "Charles Lindbergh Proved Earth Flat" —headline, *Flat Earth News*

List II

A. "Roses are red, violets are purple. Sugar is sweet and so's maple surple."
—"Dang Me"
Roger Miller

B. "The boss yelled at Joe. Joe yelled at his wife, Sue. Sue yelled at their son, Johnnie. Johnnie yelled at the dog, Spot."

C. "Brutus is an honorable man."
—*Julius Caesar*
Shakespeare

D. "I believe it is peace in our time." —Chamberlain, in 1938

E. "Breathes there a man with soul so dead, who never to himself hath said, 'This is my own, my native land.'" —Scott, "Lay of the Last Minstrel"

F. "Sometimes I sits and thinks. Sometimes I just sits." —Satchel Paige

Answers:
1. E—These two quotes express the same motive: patriotism.
2. C—These quotes are descriptions of characters.
3. F—Both are in dialect.
4. A—These quotes are parodies of other poems.
5. B—Both express cause-and-effect relationships.
6. D—These are opinions. Neither can be supported by fact.

CHECK YOUR
ANSWERS

Chapter
Four
Reading

This program guides us onward in our travels behind the scenes and into the minds of the authors and their characters.

We'll start with "The Secret Life of Walter Mitty" by James Thurber. We'll try to find out what kind of man Walter Mitty really is.

Two characters created by the same writer, Leon Driskell, appear in this program, and we see how characterization works.

After that, fiction and nonfiction excerpts demonstrate style and tone.

Goal-Setting Exercise for Program 4

Read this excerpt from *The Glass Menagerie* by Tennessee Williams and answer the questions.

Background:

Amanda, the mother, has just discovered that her daughter, Laura, has not been attending business college as she had supposed. Amanda, according to previous dialogue, was very popular when she was young. She has difficulty understanding her shy daughter.

(Laura draws a long breath and gets awkwardly to her feet. She crosses to the victrola and winds it up.)

Amanda:	What are you doing?
Laura:	Oh! *(She releases the handle and returns to her seat.)*
Amanda:	Laura, where have you been going when you've gone out pretending that you were going to business college?
Laura:	I've been out walking.
Amanda:	That's not true!
Laura:	It is. I just went walking.
Amanda:	Walking? Walking? In winter? Deliberately courting pneumonia in that light coat? Where did you walk to, Laura?
Laura:	All sorts of places—mostly in the park.
Amanda:	Even after you started catching cold?
Laura:	It was the lesser of two evils, mother. I couldn't go back up. I—threw up—on the floor!
Amanda:	From half past seven till after five every day you mean to tell me you walked around the park, because you wanted to make me think that you were still going to Rubicon's Business College?
Laura:	It wasn't as bad as it sounds. I went inside places to get warmed up.
Amanda:	Inside where?
Laura:	I went to the art museum and the bird-houses at the Zoo. I visited the penguins every day! I did without lunch and went to the movies. Lately I've been spending most of my afternoons in the Jewel-box, that big glass house where they raise tropical flowers.
Amanda:	You did all this to deceive me, just for deception? *(Laura looks down.)* Why?

Goal-Setting Exercise for Program 4 (continued)

Laura: Mother, when you're disappointed, you get that awful suffering look on your face, like the picture of Jesus's mother in the museum.

Amanda: Hush!

Now answer these questions.

1. Where did Laura go instead of attending school?
   1) bird-house, college, zoo
   2) park, art museum, Jewel-box
   3) to the movies, to visit penguins
   4) Rubicon's and art museum
   5) 2) and 3) but not 1)

1. ① ② ③ ④ ⑤

2. Laura wasn't attending college because
   1) she didn't like it
   2) it made her sick
   3) she was embarrassed
   4) she was too shy
   5) all of the above

2. ① ② ③ ④ ⑤

3. Which of the following best tells what Laura had been doing?
   1) walking in the park
   2) going to the zoo
   3) pretending to go to school, then going elsewhere
   4) deceiving her mother
   5) all of the above

3. ① ② ③ ④ ⑤

4. Amanda thought Laura was
   1) intentionally deceiving her
   2) just being stubborn
   3) lying about where she had been
   4) going to college
   5) all of the above

4. ① ② ③ ④ ⑤

**Goal-
Setting
Exercise
for
Program 4**
(continued)

5. Laura felt that she   5. ① ② ③ ④ ⑤
   1) wasn't deceiving, merely doing what she
      had to do
   2) was putting one over on her mother
   3) was having a good time
   4) 1) and 2) but not 3)
   5) 2) and 3) but not 1)

6. "Up tight" is an expression that best applies   6. ① ② ③ ④ ⑤
   to
   1) Amanda
   2) Laura
   3) Laura's brother
   4) 1) and 2) but not 3)
   5) none of these characters

Answers:

1. 5	2. 5	3. 3
4. 5	5. 1	6. 4

CHECK YOUR
ANSWERS

❏ If you got them **all right** …   SUPER. Now enjoy the program, but
                                           try to identify the shades of feeling
                                           expressed by the authors.

❏ If you missed number **1** …   Be alert to the ways authors work
                                           details into stories.

❏ If you missed number **2** …   These *details* weren't stated in one
                                           place in the story. Try to recognize the
                                           way writers give you a little informa-
                                           tion at a time and how it accumulates
                                           as the story continues.

Viewing Prescription for Program 4 (continued)

❑ If you missed number **3** ...

Be careful of implied meanings. Review the section in Chapter Two about *inferring main ideas*.

❑ If you missed number **4** ...

Watch the program with your mind tuned in to how an author tells you *what kind of person a character is*.

❑ If you missed number **5** ...

Be alert to the *implied motives* of the characters in the program.

❑ If you missed number **6** ...

What are the *feelings and emotions* of the characters in the program?

Vocabulary for Program 4

dialogue (DIE-uh-log) is what characters say. Dialogue is used in many ways, depending on the type of writing and what the author wishes to accomplish with the character.

alliteration (uh-lit-uhr-AY-shun) is the use of a series of words that all start with the same sound. "Peter Piper picked a peck of pickled peppers" is a tongue twister based on alliteration.

colloquial (coe-LOW-kwee-uhl) is everyday, even incorrect, language used in certain places. Colloquial language is used by authors to create believable characters and settings.

style (STILE) is the manner in which the author blends words and expressions to create a desired impression or feeling. Style is much easier to demonstrate that it is to define.

rhyme (RIME) is usually associated with poetry. It refers to the end sounds of words. <u>Jam</u> and <u>ham</u> rhyme. Rhyme is not a necessary element of poetry. Rhyme can be found in all sorts of reading material.

LEARN THE WORDS

Now Watch Program 4

**Subject
Matter
Review**

In order to practice skills from this program, let's continue the story of Laura and Amanda in *The Glass Menagerie*.

PRACTICE
THE SKILLS

Amanda:	**So what are we going to do with the rest of our lives? Stay home and watch the parades go by? Amuse ourselves with the glass menagerie, darling? Eternally play those worn-out phonographic records your father left as a painful reminder of him?**
	We won't have a business career—we've given that up because it gave us nervous indigestion! *(Laughs wearily.)* **What is left but dependency all our lives? I know so well what becomes of unmarried women who aren't prepared to occupy a position. I've seen such pitiful cases in the South—barely tolerated spinsters living upon the grudging patronage of sister's husband or brother's wife!—stuck away in some little mouse-trap of a room—encouraged by one in-law to visit another—little birdlike women without any nest—eating the crust of humility all their life! Isn't a very pleasant alternative, is it?**
	Of course, some girls *do* marry. *(Laura twists her hands nervously.)* **Haven't you ever liked a boy?**
Laura:	**Yes, I liked one once.** *(Rises.)* **I came across his picture a while ago.**
Amanda:	*(With some interest.)* **He gave you a picture?**
Laura:	**No, it's in the year-book.**
Amanda:	*(Disappointed.)* **Oh—a high school boy.**
(Screen image: Jim as a high school hero bearing a silver cup.)	
Laura:	**Yes, his name was Jim.** *(Laura lifts the heavy annual from the claw-foot table.)* **Here he is in *The Pirates of Penzance*.**
Amanda:	**The what?**
Laura:	**The operetta the senior class put on. He had a wonderful voice and we sat across the aisle from each other Mondays, Wednesdays, and Fridays in the Aud. Here he is with the silver cup for debating! See his grin?**
Amanda:	*(Absently.)* **He must have had a jolly disposition.**
Laura:	**He used to call me—Blue Roses.**
Amanda:	**Why did he call you such a name as that?**
Laura:	**When I had that attack of pleurosis—he thought I said Blue Roses! So that's what he'd always call me after that. Whenever he saw me, he'd holler, "Hello, Blue**

Roses!" I didn't care for the girl that he went with Emily Meisenbach. Emily was the best dressed girl at Soldan. She never struck me, though, as being sincere.... It says in the Personal Section—they're engaged. That's six years ago! They must be married by now.

Amanda: Girls that aren't cut out for business careers usually wind up married to some nice man. *(Gets up, with a spark of revival.)* Sister, that's what you'll do!

(Laura utters a startled, doubtful laugh. She reaches quickly for a glass animal from the shelf.)

Laura: But Mother—

Amanda: Yes? *(Crossing to photograph.)*

Laura: *(In a tone of frightened apology.)* I'm crippled!

Now answer these questions.

1. In Amanda's first speech, she uses "we" and   1.① ② ③ ④ ⑤
   "us." To whom is she referring?
   1) herself and her daughter
   2) herself, her daughter, and her son
   3) herself only
   4) her daughter only
   5) many women

2. Who does Amanda think will spend a lifetime   2.① ② ③ ④ ⑤
   going from one relative to another?
   1) Amanda
   2) Laura
   3) Amanda and Laura
   4) Laura's brother
   5) Laura's father

3. Amanda was disappointed because the picture   3.① ② ③ ④ ⑤
   of Jim was
   1) a high school boy
   2) not given to Laura by Jim
   3) a bad likeness
   4) a picture of him in costume
   5) all of the above

4. It can be inferred from this passage that   4. ① ② ③ ④ ⑤
   1) Jim "liked" Laura.
   2) Jim knew Laura but it was Laura who
      "liked" Jim.
   3) Emily wasn't well liked in school.
   4) Jim was not well liked at school.
   5) Laura was very popular.

5. Which of the following best describes the   5. ① ② ③ ④ ⑤
   relationships implied in this scene?
   1) Laura wasn't very popular.
   2) Jim was in love with Laura.
   3) Emily liked Laura.
   4) Jim and Laura would have married if it
      hadn't been for Emily.
   5) Laura was as popular as Jim.

6. Amanda says, "Eternally play those worn-out
   phonographic records your father left as a
   painful reminder of him?" From the tone of
   this speech, what do you think happened to
   Laura's father?

   _____

   _____

   _____

   _____

   _____

   _____

   _____

7. Amanda says, "little bird-like *women* without
   any nest—eating the crust of humility all
   their *life*!" "Women" isn't a parallel expression to "life." You would expect "women" to
   go with "lives." Why did the author select
   these words to go together?

   _____

   _____

   _____

   _____

   _____

   _____

   _____

CHECK YOUR
ANSWERS

**Subject
Matter
Review
(continued)**

Answers:
1. 4—Amanda was using **sarcasm**. She is really talking about Laura.
2. 2—She's threatening Laura by telling her how miserable she'll be.
3. 2—Amanda makes a distinction between a picture "given" and "just a picture in a yearbook." If the boy had "given" Laura his picture, this would imply a deeper relationship.
4. 2—Knowing about high school people, you can infer that it was Laura who "liked" Jim. It's unlikely he had those same feelings about Laura. He was popular, and this usually means friendly. It would also be logical to infer that Laura fantasized about Jim.
5. 1—There's nothing to indicate that Jim loved Laura, so 2 is out. By the same thinking, 4 and 5 aren't any good. There's nothing to suggest how Emily feels about Laura, so 3 isn't the best answer. What you do know is that Laura is a sickly, shy cripple. These character traits don't usually make a high school youth popular.
6. Nothing in what you read tells for certain, but he is only referred to in the play. You know he isn't around.
7. It is a way to show something about Amanda's character. She makes general statements and applies them to Laura.

Detecting Purpose, Viewpoint, and Attitudes

**LEARN THE
SKILLS**

Sometimes it is difficult to understand the purpose of a story or the attitude of a character or writer. To help yourself understand, try to answer these three basic questions as often as possible.

What is it?

What's it about?

How do I know?

When you have the story firmly in mind, ask these two additional questions: "What did the character do (say, think, feel) about it?" and "What would I do (say, think, feel) about the same or a similar situation?"

Here is "The Secret Life of Walter Mitty" retold to answer these questions.

(What is it?)

It's a story …

(What's it about?)

About a weak man who was threatened by a strong wife.

(How do I know?)

The story says (or implies) that …

(What did the character do?)

… he retreated into a fantasy world rather than face his problems.

(What would I do about the same or a similar situation?)

_____
_____
_____
_____
_____
_____
_____
_____

"The Secret Life of Walter Mitty" appeals to readers because so many people do exactly the same thing Walter Mitty did.

Keep this simple formula in mind. We'll use it again to find out other hidden information.

What you believe, even your upbringing, will affect the way you translate this passage. Keep an open mind and try to see different points of view.

PRACTICE THE SKILLS

> **A high school student had just won a National Award of Excellence for his essay, which compared the writings of J.D. Salinger to various passages in the Bible. He was totally unprepared for the reaction of his hometown. He had expected a hero's homecoming, but it was not to be.**
>
> **Irate parents stormed the high school library. They raided the public library and several bookstores, removed and burned dozens of copies of the J.D. Salinger classic *Catcher in the Rye*. These actions were prompted by what their leaders said was "indignation over the school encouraging our young people to read such a filthy book."**
>
> **Librarians and bookshop owners threatened lawsuits. They claimed that the book was of accepted literary value and to remove it was a violation of freedom of speech.**
>
> **The school board held several uncomfortable hearings on "pornography in the schools."**

Before you answer the questions, try to evaluate this article using the questioning process described in the Skill Helpers. We'll get you started.

(What is it?)
   It's an article …

(What's it about?)
   … about a controversy

(What is it? What's it about? [The controversy, that is.])

_____

_____

_____

(How do I know?)

_____

_____

_____

(What did the characters do?)

_____

_____

_____

(What would I do in the same or a similar situation?)

_____

_____

_____

_____

Now answer these questions.

1. Who is right in this controversy?

   _____

   _____

2. Should the parents have burned the books? Explain your answer.

   _____

   _____

   _____

   _____

3. Were the parents' actions a violation of Constitutional rights?

   _____

   _____

   _____

   _____

4. How would you have handled this situation if you had been one of the irate parents? The student's teacher? A bookshop owner?

   _____

   _____

   _____

   _____

   _____

   _____

   _____

   _____

Answers:
This section has no correct answers. All answers will differ because they reflect opinions.

CHECK YOUR ANSWERS

Just for Fun

Here's a little insanity that gives you an opportunity to think up movie or TV titles and decide who starred in the show. The game was inspired by rock star Frank Zappa, who calls the family canary "BIRD Reynolds." Example:

The movie *Fuzz in My Pocket* starring LINT Eastwood (It's about a corrupt policeman.)

This one may need a little explanation. "Fuzz" is slang for policeman. Fuzz is also lint. The expression "to have someone in your pocket" means you are bribing them. Of course, Clint Eastwood is often associated with films about policemen.

Got it? Here's one more: the movie *Furniture Factory* starring CHAIR Bono. Now here is a list of movies and the like. Tell who you think stars in each one.

```
A movie: Operating Room starring
A movie: Over the Falls starring
A stereo album: The Last Great Songs of
A documentary: The Reluctant Boxer narrated by
A music video: "I Lost My Glove in a Tower in
    Paris" starring
```

Once you get the pattern, you can make up your own. Don't expect your friends to think they're as funny as you think they are.

Answers:
Here are our suggestions: *Operating Room* starring Sterile Burnette (Carol); *Over the Falls* starring Barrel Streep (Meryl); *The Last Great Songs of Final Richie* (Lionel); *The Reluctant Boxer* narrated by Coward Cosell (Howard); "I Lost My Glove in a Tower in Paris" starring Eiffel Jackson (Michael).

CHECK YOUR ANSWERS

Test-Taking Tip

Answers on GED tests tend to parallel the form of the question. This means the answer must be the same kind of word or phrase. Example:

My brother loves stamps so much he <u>collects</u> them.

Which of the following words would best replace <u>collects</u> in the sentence above?
1) **accumulate**
2) **hoard**
3) **amass**
4) **saves**

4 is the answer. Its form is parallel. Try saying the other words in the place of <u>collects</u>. They don't sound right.

Skills Checklist

This lesson has dealt with characters and their moods, emotions, and motives. Make a list of the characters you remember from the video and the workbook exercises. Make a very short statement of their most memorable traits.

Read this selection and answer the questions.

EXTRA
PRACTICE

> **George Ripley, Bronson Alcott, Ralph Waldo Emerson, and Henry D. Thoreau were the originators or "re-inventors" of the Transcendental theory, the belief that human experience could be surpassed but the limits of the mind could not.**
>
> **Thoreau frequently put the theory to the test by acting out the philosophy. He refused to pay $1.25 in poll tax on the grounds it was wrong to "… buy a musket and hire a man to use this musket to kill another." Alcott had previously made similar seditious statements. The authorities feared insurrection, and Thoreau was thrown in jail.**
>
> **Emerson went to visit the incarcerated Thoreau and said, "Henry, why are you in here?"**
>
> **"Waldo, why are you *not* in here?" asked Thoreau. For Emerson, the play on words hit too close to home, so he let Thoreau spend the night in jail.**
>
> **Thoreau's desire to savor the victory was short-lived because someone, presumably Emerson, paid his fine and he was released the next morning.**

1. <u>Transcendental</u> means   1. ① ② ③ ④ ⑤
   1) a theory that says thought is supreme
   2) doing is more important than thinking
   3) war is immoral
   4) taxes should not be paid if you don't
      agree with the way the money is spent
   5) action speaks louder than words

2. Which of the following best replaces   2. ① ② ③ ④ ⑤
   <u>seditious</u>?
   1) unpopular
   2) unfavorable
   3) unpatriotic
   4) unhappy
   5) unpleasant

3. <u>Incarcerated</u> means to be   3. ① ② ③ ④ ⑤
   1) terminally ill
   2) afraid
   3) very unhappy
   4) in confinement
   5) visiting

4. Which of the following words best replaces   4. ① ② ③ ④ ⑤
   <u>insurrection</u>?
   1) rebellious
   2) rebellion
   3) civil disorder
   4) 1) and 3) but not 2)
   5) 2) and 3) but not 1)

5. The authorities thought that   5. ① ② ③ ④ ⑤
   1) Alcott and Thoreau were trying to cause
       trouble
   2) Thoreau should be jailed for non-payment
       of the tax
   3) Thoreau was a criminal
   4) 1) and 2)
   5) 2) and 3)

6. Thoreau thought   6. ① ② ③ ④ ⑤
   1) his taxes should not be used to kill
       people
   2) Emerson was not sincere enough in his
       beliefs
   3) thinking is OK but you need to do the
       things you believe
   4) all of the above
   5) none of the above

Subject
Matter
Review
(continued)

7. Which of the following is *not* what Emerson thought?

   1) Thinking is the most important thing in the world.

   2) Thoreau should not have let himself be arrested.

   3) Thoreau was impertinent and should be taught a lesson.

   4) Thoreau should stay in jail to make a statement about his philosophy.

   5) 3) and 4)

7. ① ② ③ ④ ⑤

8. What "victory" did Thoreau wish to savor?

_____

_____

_____

_____

_____

_____

9. How do you know the men in this story were not the first to hold this philosophy?

_____

_____

_____

_____

_____

_____

Answers:

1. 1   2. 3   3. 4   4. 5

5. 4   6. 4   7. 4

8. Thoreau thought that being in jail would attract attention to his cause.

9. The article says they were "re-inventors," which implies someone else had invented it before.

CHECK YOUR
ANSWERS

Chapter Five
Reading

Now we are ready to apply our reading skills to materials you might not consider a part of reading. Charts, graphs, maps, and cartoons are important ways we communicate with each other, but learning to read them requires practice.

The video starts with a discussion of globes and how they represent the world. "Reading" a globe helps you answer the question, "Where am I?"

Next, the program introduces maps for specialized purposes. Road maps, city maps, and even the kind you see on television weather reports have their own characteristics and must be understood if you are to get full value from them.

The program then takes up graphs, charts, and tables. These visuals occupy a great deal of space in most popular reading material. Magazines and books, even salespeople who want to prove a point use these tools to organize information.

Most visuals have much information packed into a small space. This program will show you where to find it.

Goal-Setting Exercise for Program 5

Study the map of northern New Mexico and answer the questions.

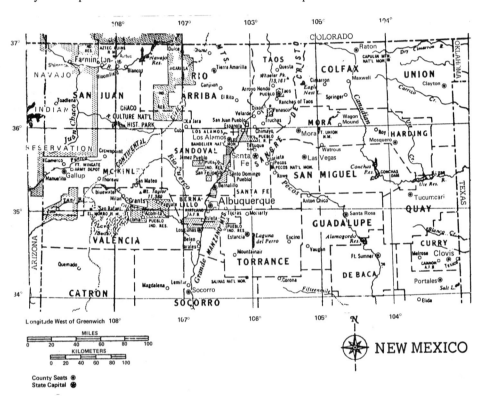

Now answer these questions.

1. Which of the following tells the approximate location of the town Socorro, NM?   1.① ② ③ ④ ⑤
   1) 34°N lat. 107°E long.
   2) 34°N lat. 107°W long.
   3) 34°N lat. 36°W long.
   4) 34°E lat. 107°S long.
   5) 34°W lat. 107°W long.

2. Which of these is the state capital?   2.① ② ③ ④ ⑤
   1) Tucumcari
   2) Los Alamos
   3) Santa Fe
   4) Gallup
   5) Portales

Goal-Setting Exercise for Program 5 (continued)

3. Which of the following are almost exactly   3. ① ② ③ ④ ⑤
   east and west of each other?
   1) Mora and Las Vegas
   2) Watrous and Mosquero
   3) Mosquero and Tucumcari
   4) Rio Arriba County and San Miguel County
   5) Santa Rosa and Mosquero

4. How far is it from Santa Fe to Maxwell?   4. ① ② ③ ④ ⑤
   1) 100 miles   .
   2) 160 kilometers
   3) 250 kilometers
   4) 1) and 2) but not 3)
   5) 2) and 3) but not 1)

5. Gallup, Aztec, Clayton, and Tucumcari are all   5. ① ② ③ ④ ⑤
   1) the same distance from Santa Fe
   2) south of 34° lat.
   3) west of 106°W long.
   4) county seats
   5) all of the above

Study the graph below and answer the questions.

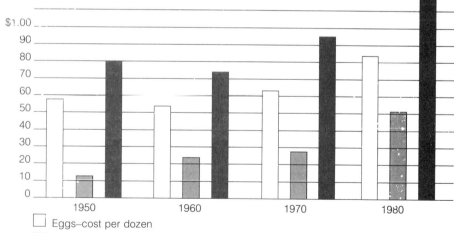

Eggs–cost per dozen
Bread–cost per pound
Coffee–cost per pound

Goal-Setting Exercise for Program 5 (continued)

Now answer these questions.

6. What was the cost of coffee per pound in   6. ① ② ③ ④ ⑤
   1950?
   1)   90 cents
   2)   15 cents
   3)   80 cents
   4)   57 cents
   5)   75 cents

7. In what years were the egg prices most simi-   7. ① ② ③ ④ ⑤
   lar?
   1)   1950 and 1960
   2)   1960 and 1970
   3)   1970 and 1980
   4)   1950 and 1970
   5)   1960 and 1980

8. Which of the following can be inferred from   8. ① ② ③ ④ ⑤
   this graph?
   1)   Prices increased fairly gradually until
        1980.
   2)   The great increase in price of coffee in
        1980 is out of proportion to the other
        years.
   3)   Bread has remained almost the same price
        for four decades.
   4)   1) and 2) but not 3)
   5)   3) and 1) but not 2)

Answers for Goal-Setting Exercise:

1. 2	2. 3	3. 2	4. 4
5. 4	6. 3	7. 1	8. 4

CHECK YOUR
ANSWERS

Viewing Prescription for Program 5

❑ If you got them **all right** …

SUPER. When you watch the video, try to pick up a few things you don't already know.

❑ If you missed number **1** …

Pay close attention to the discussion of *longitude* and *latitude*.

❑ If you missed number **2** or **3** …

Watch for clues about finding *details* in visuals.

❑ If you missed number **4** or **5** …

Be sure you pay attention to how to read *legends*.

❑ If you missed number **6** or **7** …

Visuals are an easy means of *comparing and contrasting* information. See how often this idea comes up in the video presentation and study the workbook examples carefully.

❑ If you missed number **8** …

One purpose for using visuals is so you can make quick *inferences*. The video should help you with this skill.

Vocabulary for Program 5

caricature (KARE-uh-kuh-chure) is an exaggerated or distorted drawing.

hemisphere (HEM-iss-fear) means "half the ball" and refers to a section of the globe. The world can be divided into eastern and western or northern and southern hemispheres.

latitude (LAT-uh-tude) imaginary lines that run around the globe parallel to the equator. These lines are called *parallels* because they are always the same distance apart.

longitude (LONJ-uh-tude) imaginary lines on the globe that cross the parallels. Called *meridians*, longitude lines are not parallel because they meet at the poles.

LEARN THE
WORDS

Vocabulary for Program 5 (continued)

axis (AX-iss) is a point around which something turns. The Earth's axis is imaginary, but useful when we talk about how the Earth turns.

axis is also used to talk about graphs. In graphs, the lines containing information are drawn on verical and horizontal axes.

grid (GRID) A network of lines or bars that divide a map or globe into sections.

coordinates (koh-ORD-uh-nuhts) Points on a grid where lines cross.

scale (SKALE) The relationship between real distance or size and the size or distance of a map or model.

legend (LEJ-und) gives the scale, symbols, and other information needed to read a map, chart, etc.

relief (re-LEAF) Some maps depict the surface of the ground. Such maps, which tell the elevation and show *contours* of mountains and valleys, are called "relief maps."

Now Watch Program 5

Subject Matter Review

Here are some of the things you should have learned from the program.

About Globes and Maps

1. The equator is an imaginary line running around the globe halfway between the north and south poles.
2. Latitude lines on the globe are called parallels because they go around the globe the same direction as the equator and are *always* the same distance apart.
3. Globes are also divided by longitude lines called meridians. These lines run from pole to pole. Meridians *are not* parallel.
4. Any point on Earth can be defined by telling its position in relation to the latitude and longitude grid.
5. Zero longitude runs through Greenwich, England. The equator is zero latitude.
6. Latitude and longitude are measured in degrees (minutes and seconds) from the starting point. Longitude is stated in degrees east or west of Greenwich. Latitude is stated in degrees north or south of the equator.

LEARN THE FACTS

Use the map of northern New Mexico at the beginning of the chapter to answer the following questions.

PRACTICE THE SKILLS

1. Which of these towns is located on the Navajo Indian Reservation?
   1) Portales
   2) Clayton
   3) Shiprock
   4) Socorro
   5) Albuquerque

1. ① ② ③ ④ ⑤

2. Which of these states is on the northern border of New Mexico?
   1) Colorado
   2) Georgia
   3) Arizona
   4) Oklahoma
   5) Texas

2. ① ② ③ ④ ⑤

3. Which of the following is a mountain range?   3. ① ② ③ ④ ⑤
   1) DeBaca
   2) Rio Puerco
   3) Wagon Mound
   4) Pecos
   5) Manzano

4. Which of these rivers runs near the town of   4. ① ② ③ ④ ⑤
   Santa Rosa?
   1) Grande
   2) Canadian
   3) Juan Chaco
   4) Rio Puerco
   5) Pecos

Answers:

1. 3   2. 1   3. 5   4. 5

CHECK YOUR ANSWERS

Graphs

Like maps, some graphs use **coordinates**. Just as maps use reference points to locate positions, graphs use coordinates to compare two or more related bits of information.

The following graph uses a line to compare U.S. and Soviet space flights over a period of time. The number of space flights is listed on the *horizontal axis*, and the years are shown on the *vertical axis*. The graph includes a *legend* to tell you the meanings of the` symbols.

MANNED SPACE FLIGHT
1961 to 1982

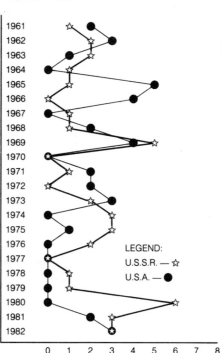

LEGEND:
U.S.S.R. — ☆
U.S.A. — ●

LEARN THE SKILLS

Subject
Matter
Review
(continued)

Now answer these questions.

**PRACTICE
THE SKILLS**

1. In what year were the most total flights made
   (U.S. and USSR together)?
   1) 1970
   2) 1980
   3) 1969
   4) 1964
   5) 1971

1.① ② ③ ④ ⑤

2. Which of the following can you conclude from
   this graph?
   1) The U.S. has the most advanced space
       vehicles.
   2) A total of 183 flights has been made by
       both countries.
   3) The USSR made a few more flights than the
       U.S. during this period.
   4) The USSR is winning the space race.
   5) The number of yearly space flights by
       both countries has been fairly even
       throughout the years.

2.① ② ③ ④ ⑤

3. Which of the following pairs of years had the
   least space activity?
   1) 1961 and 1977
   2) 1978 and 1979
   3) 1970 and 1977
   4) 1976 and 1977
   5) 1975 and 1979

3.① ② ③ ④ ⑤

Answers:

1. 3   2. 5   3. 3

**CHECK YOUR
ANSWERS**

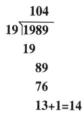

Subject Matter Review (continued)

Now read this passage and answer the questions below.

PRACTICE THE SKILLS

How To Use the Paschal Full Moon Chart

The information in this chart is the basis for the determination of the exact date of Easter.

There are 19 cycles of the Paschal Full Moon. The year in question is divided by 19. One is then added to the remainder to arrive at the Golden Number, which tells the date of the PFM. Easter is the next Sunday after this date. If the PFM falls on a Sunday, Easter is the next Sunday.

Example: What is the date of Easter in 1989?

```
        104
   19)1989
      19
        89
        76
      13+1=14
```

The Golden Number for 1989 is 14.

The chart shows that the date corresponding to the Golden Number 14 is March 22, which falls on Wednesday. Easter is the next Sunday, or March 26.

Paschal Full Moon Dates 1900 to 2199

Golden Number	Date	Golden Number	Date
1	Apr. 14	10	Apr. 5
2	Apr. 3	11	Mar. 25
3	Mar. 23	12	Apr. 13
4	Apr. 11	13	Apr. 2
5	Mar. 31	14	Mar. 22
6	Apr. 18	15	Apr. 10
7	Apr. 8	16	Mar. 30
8	Mar. 28	17	Apr. 17
9	Apr. 16	18	Apr. 7
		19	Mar. 27

1. The PMF for the year 1999 is:
   1) April 11
   2) March 27
   3) April 5
   4) April 3
   5) March 31

1. ① ② ③ ④ ⑤

**Subject
Matter
Review**
(continued)

2. The date of Easter in the year 1999 will be: 2.① ② ③ ④ ⑤
   1) April 18
   2) March 31
   3) April 3
   4) April 5
   5) There isn't enough information given to
       be sure.

3. The folk saying, "Easter falls on the first   3.① ② ③ ④ ⑤
   Sunday after the first full moon after the
   spring equinox," tells when Easter is. Using
   this saying, what is the date of Easter in
   the year 2004?
   1) March 31
   2) April 11
   3) April 3
   4) March 28
   5) There isn't enough information given to
       be sure.

4. The first full moon after the spring equinox   4.① ② ③ ④ ⑤
   is the same as
   1) the first day of spring
   2) the harvest moon
   3) the Paschal Full Moon
   4) the date of Easter
   5) There isn't enough information given to
       be sure.

5. What other information do we need to answer   5.① ② ③ ④ ⑤
   Questions 2 and 3?
   1) the date of the first Easter
   2) the day of the week of the full moon
   3) the day of the week of the equinox
   4) the date of the harvest moon
   5) Paschal's full name

Answers:
1. 5   2. 5   3. 5   4. 3
5. 2—Notice that the day of the week is given in the explanation.

CHECK YOUR
ANSWERS

**Subject
Matter
Review**
(continued)

LEARN THE
SKILLS

Cartoons

You can use the same questioning process to evaluate cartoons as you used in Chapter Four to evaluate purpose.

Start by simply asking: What is it? What's it about? How do I know?

With cartoons, you may need to ask one more question: What's behind the cartoon that I have to understand?"

"I won't collect any more rent from Franz Mesmer, I won't collect any
more rent from Franz Mesmer . . . "

Look at this cartoon. Its purpose is to make you laugh. Do you think it's funny?

Evaluate it like this:

(What is it?)

It's a cartoon …

(What's it about?)

… about a man who has hypnotized his landlord so he won't be billed for his rent.

(What's behind the cartoon that I have to understand?)

Franz Mesmer is the person who discovered hypnotism.

Cartoons frequently deal with human weaknesses or some other hidden meaning. Sometimes they refer to incidents or ideas you must understand before the cartoons make any sense. Read this selection and answer the questions.

Cartoons have a powerful impact on the way we think about ourselves and our world. When a person is called a "Bumstead," he

PRACTICE
THE SKILLS

Subject Matter Review (continued)

is being compared to the character in "Dagwood and Blondie."

Thomas Nast's pen hurried the downfall of the Tammany Hall political machine. The simple, almost crude, understated art of James Thurber caused us to smile at our weaknesses. Walt Kelly made us wonder whether Pogo was funny or philosophical. Pogo even ran for president.

Snoopy became a latter-day Walter Mitty, and all of Schultz's Peanuts made us yearn for the saner world of a child. Doonesbury moved from the comic page to the editorial page, and Garfield took his place as everyone's favorite "fat cat."

Cartoon characters are keen observers of the passing scene. Their satire points out the weaknesses we have chosen to overlook. They teach us in a way we don't resent. In fact, we love them for it. We understand ourselves better because of them.

Now answer these questions.

1. The first paragraph is mainly about   1. ① ② ③ ④ ⑤
   1) cartoon characters
   2) cartoonists
   3) the way cartoons have become a part of our language
   4) the way we associate ideas with cartoon-ists
   5) Dagwood Bumstead and Rube Goldberg

2. Which of the following proverbs best de- 2. ① ② ③ ④ ⑤
   scribes the second paragraph?
   1) Don't cry over spilled milk.
   2) The pen is mightier than the sword.
   3) Make hay while the sun shines.
   4) He who hesitates is lost.
   5) One good turn deserves another.

3. The third paragraph implies   3. ① ② ③ ④ ⑤
   1) Cartoon satire makes us angry.
   2) Doonesbury isn't funny.
   3) Snoopy, Doonesbury, and Garfield have a lot in common.
   4) Doonesbury is more like Garfield than Peanuts.
   5) Peanuts cartoons offer escape from the reality of everyday life.

Study these cartoons.

A.
Automatic Sheet Music Turner

At last! The great brain of the distinguished man of science gives the world the simple automatic sheet music turner!

Press left foot (**A**) on pedal (**B**) which pulls down handle (**C**) on tire pump (**D**). Pressure of air blows whistle (**E**)–goldfish (**F**) believes this is dinner signal and starts feeding on worm (**G**). The pull on string (**H**) releases brace (**I**), dropping shelf (**J**), leaving weight (**K**) without support. Naturally, hatrack (**L**) is suddenly extended and boxing glove (**M**) hits punching bag (**N**) which, in turn, is punctured by spike (**O**).

Escaping air blows against sail (**P**) which is attached to page of music (**Q**), which turns gently and makes way for the next outburst of sweet or sour melody.

B.

DANA SUMMERS
Courtesy The Sentinel

C.

"Peterson, it isn't necessary for you to tell your passengers that your name is Walter Peterson and that you'll be their pilot for the entire trip."

Subject Matter Review (continued)

Below is a list of statements which may or may not be the points the cartoonists were trying to make.

1. People see problems rather than solutions.
2. People complain but don't act.
3. People try to make themselves more important then they really are.
4. People feel that there is always someone to tell them what to do.
5. Society relies on elaborate institutions to solve its problems.
6. People identify many problems of society that don't need to be solved.
7. People feel as if they are not in control of their lives.

4. Which of the numbered traits listed above best apply to cartoon A?
   1) 1, 3, and 4
   2) 5, 6, and 7
   3) 5 and 6 but not 7
   4) 1 but not 3 and 4
   5) 2 and 4 only

4. ① ② ③ ④ ⑤

5. Which of the numbered traits best apply to Cartoon B?
   1) 1 and 2
   2) 1, 2, 3, and 4
   3) 4 and 5
   4) 4, 5, and 6
   5) 1, 2, and 7

5. ① ② ③ ④ ⑤

6. Which of the numbered traits best apply to Cartoon C?
   1) 1 and 2
   2) 2 and 3
   3) 3 and 4
   4) 4 and 5
   5) 6 and 7

6. ① ② ③ ④ ⑤

Answers:

1. 3	2. 2	3. 5
4. 2	5. 5	6. 3

CHECK YOUR ANSWERS

Just for Fun

1. A man built a square house with windows on all four sides, all of them facing south. One day a bear came to his door. What color was the bear?

2. Joe was visiting a very systematized country. He saw a signpost which told the number of miles to many cities. The sign was old and he couldn't read some of the distances. He could see that he was four miles from Dibble, eight miles from Harbyxt, and 26 miles from Zandinglet. How far was he from these cities?

   Abraxax   _____
   Minnote   _____
   Pyrenairy   _____
   Lundle   _____
   Waxington   _____
   (Clue: It's one mile to Abraxax.)

Answers:
1. White. The only place on Earth where it's possible to have a southern exposure on all sides of your house is at the North Pole, where white polar bears live.
2. The distance to each city matches the alphabetical position of the name's first letter. Minnote is 13 miles, Lundle is 12 miles, Pyreniary is 16 miles, and Waxington is 23 miles.

CHECK YOUR ANSWERS

Test-Taking Tip

When answering questions about maps, charts, or graphs, be sure you use only the information given to make your judgment. A graph can easily show something that you know to be untrue. Nevertheless, answer the question as if the information were correct. Example:

City Sales Tax Rates
For these selected cities, the first rate given is the state rate. The second is the city or county rate.

City	Sales Tax Rates
Atlanta	3%+1%
Birmingham	4%+1%
Buffalo	4%+3%
Cincinnati	4%+1/2%
Denver	3%+3%

1. **Which of the following cities has the lowest combined state and city tax?**
    1) **Buffalo**
    2) **Cincinnati**
    3) **Denver**
    4) **Atlanta**
    5) **Birmingham**

Suppose you live in Atlanta and you know that the rate in that city has been increased to 5%, so you answer the question: 2. Your answer would be wrong because the increase is not shown on the chart. *On charts and graphs, make your answer reflect the information given, not any additional information you might have.*

Read this fantasy and answer the questions.

EXTRA PRACTICE

Congress has passed a law saying that no state can have a population of fewer than 9 million people or more than 12 million. States with fewer than 9 million must join with their neighboring states until their combined populations fall within the prescribed limits.

States whose current populations fall within this range may keep their present boundaries. States which exceed the limits must divide their states, making two new states.

This plan drastically alters what our country looks like.

Below is a new map of the U.S. Study it and answer the questions.

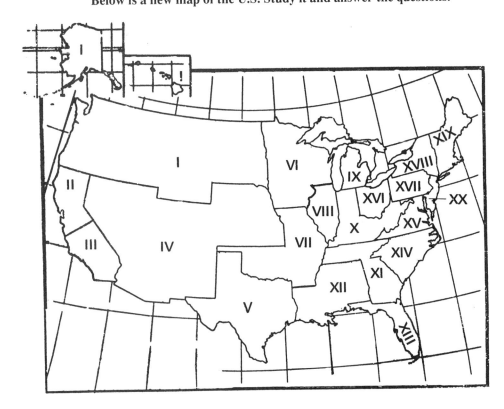

1. Many of the states look just as they did   1.① ② ③ ④ ⑤
   before the new law because
   1) it prevents confusion.
   2) there was no state near them that they
      could join with.
   3) Congress wanted it that way.
   4) their growth rate will soon cause them to
      exceed the required limit.
   5) their current population is within the
      new limits.

2. Only one state was divided into two states   2.① ② ③ ④ ⑤
   because
   1) Colorado was too big to begin with.
   2) California's current opoulation is more
      than 18 million.
   3) Utah has experienced great population
      growth.
   4) Texas is losing population rapidly.
   5) Vermont has a stable population.

3. According to additional rules, the states are   3.① ② ③ ④ ⑤
   to be numbered instead of named and state
   capitals will be decided by lot. In order for
   a city to be considered, it must be located
   in the new state and have a current population of more than 100,000 people. Which of
   the following is *not* a new capital?
   1) Chicago, State I
   2) Denver, State IV
   3) Atlanta, State XI
   4) Columbus, State XVI
   5) Springfield, State VIII

4. What could be said about the current popula-   4.① ② ③ ④ ⑤
   tion of our country?
   1) Our population can't be less than 180
      million or more than 240 million.
   2) People in state XII are generally older
      than people in the other states.
   3) Several states already have populations
      of more than 9 million.
   4) 1) and 2) but not 3)
   5) 1) and 3) but not 2)

Subject Matter Review (continued)

Answers:
1. 5   2. 2   3. 1   4. 5

CHECK YOUR
ANSWERS

Chapter Six
Science

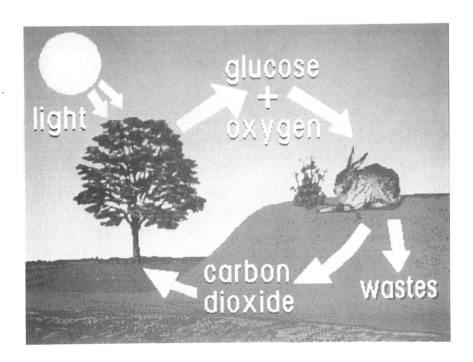

Today we get our first chance to apply our reading skills to the field of science. It will be apparent very rapidly that word skills are important in biology.

How many, how big, and how small are important questions in science, so our series starts with a brief discussion of scientific measurement. Because scientists often work with things that are terribly large or very tiny, they must have ways of making comparisons.

Pay particular attention to the "cycles" discussed. Without these complex relationships, no life would exist on Earth.

Next, the program deals with plant and animal relationships. You'll find examples of how life cooperates, competes, and changes.

As you go through the science lessons, keep these three rules in mind:

1. Nature always tries to be in balance.
2. Nothing is wasted in nature.
3. Nothing stands alone in nature.

Goal-Setting Exercise for Program 6

Read this selection and answer the questions.

Energy transfer from one form to another is terribly inefficient. One natural example after another demonstrates this principle, but humans can't seem to remember it.

Only a small portion of the solar energy stored in a plant is converted to body heat by an animal which eats the plant. A field of alfalfa, for instance, receives 4,000 times as much solar energy as it yields in caloric value when consumed.

The difference between what an organism receives and what it produces is compounded at every level of the food pyramid. Small herbivores eating the alfalfa convert less than 10% of the plant's energy into tissue and movement.

An eagle must eat several pounds of rabbit to maintain one pound of its own weight.

Eugene Odoms, in his book *Fundamentals of Ecology*, uses the following example: It takes more than 17,000 pounds of alfalfa to raise 2,250 pounds of beef. This much beef is needed to sustain one 105-pound boy.

Now answer these questions.

1. This article is mainly about   1. ① ② ③ ④ ⑤
   1) how energy is transferred from plants to animals.
   2) the loss of energy as it is changed from one form to another.
   3) the inefficiency of solar energy.
   4) how alfalfa grows.
   5) how herbivores get their energy.

2. Which of the following words best replaces   2. ① ② ③ ④ ⑤
   "caloric" in this article?
   1) sunlight
   2) heat
   3) dollar
   4) invested
   5) all of the above

Goal-Setting Exercise for Program 6 (continued)

3. "Herbivores" means animals which eat   3.① ② ③ ④ ⑤
   1) only at night
   2) meat only
   3) plants
   4) only alfalfa
   5) none of the above

4. Which of the following is *not* implied by this   4.① ② ③ ④ ⑤
   passage?
   1) The food pyramid is connected to energy
      from the sun.
   2) Humans rely on forms of life lower on the
      food pyramid.
   3) Meat eaters are more efficient than plant
      eaters.
   4) Green plants form the base of the food
      pyramid.
   5) Sunlight powers plants and the plant
      eaters.

Answers:
  1. 2   2. 2   3. 3   4. 3

CHECK YOUR
ANSWERS

Viewing Prescription for Program 6

☐ If you missed number **1** …   You may still be having difficulty
                                         with finding the ***main idea*** of a
                                         reading passage. Watch carefully as
                                         the video tells about the main idea in
                                         science material.

☐ If you missed number **2** or **3** … Be alert to what is said about ***context***
                                         clues and science material.

☐ If you missed number **4** …   You will get a lot of practice in
                                         inferring meaning. Hang in there.

Vocabulary for Program 6

abyss (uh-BIS), in this context, means a deep part of the ocean.

biology (by-AH-low-gee) is the study of life.

biological (bi-oh-LAH-gee-kuhl) refers to the study or science of biology.

symbiosis (sim-by-OH-sis) means living together. It is one of the types of living systems in nature.

species (SPEE-seez) refers to the classification of living things. Our species is *sapiens*. In biology, two names are used to refer to a specific example of life: *genus* and *species*. We are *homo sapiens*.

adaptations (a-dap-TAY-shun) means to change to take advantage of a special circumstance.

photosynthesis (foh-toe-SIN-thuh-sis) is the process by which plants make food from sunlight and chemicals.

LEARN THE WORDS

Now Watch Program 6

**Subject
Matter
Review**

Here are some bits of information you should remember from the video portion of this lesson.

1. The cycles referred to in this program rely on various kinds of cooperation in order to pass the raw materials of life from one form to another.
2. A crucial part of the living cycle is the food web.
3. Introduction of foreign substances such as DDT into the ecological cycles can drastically alter the food web.
4. Few germs are harmful; most are neutral; many are helpful.
5. Ecosystems change all the time.
6. Except for one extremely rare example, all life on Earth depends on the sun.

LEARN THE
FACTS

Living things have invented some uncanny ways of cooperating with each other. For instance, nitrogen-fixing bacteria invade the roots of certain plants. They live there and help the bacteria grow. Some algae enter the bodies of fungi to form communities called lichens.

The most interesting and befuddling examples, however, occur in the animal kingdom. Bacteria called Trichonympha live in the digestive tracts of termites. They break down cellulose so the termites can digest it. Without this teammate, a termite could eat an entire forest and starve to death.

Farming ants grow a unique strain of fungus in their underground gardens by feeding the fungus masticated leaves. This ant species is especially adapted to the fungus-growing enterprise. Virgin queens have a sac in their heads so they can take a start of the fungus along with them when they begin a new colony. This ant-fungus association is extremely close. Neither could exist without the other.

PRACTICE
THE SKILLS

Now answer these questions.

1. This passage is mainly about
   1) termites' digestive systems.
   2) the way organisms compete in nature.
   3) fungi and lichens.
   4) examples of many kinds of plants and animals.
   5) ways in which organisms cooperate in order to live.

1. ① ② ③ ④ ⑤

2. The word <u>teammate</u> in the second paragraph refers to
   1) termites
   2) trichonympha
   3) digestive tracts
   4) cellulose
   5) bacteria

2. ① ② ③ ④ ⑤

3. Gardens in new farmer ant colonies are started by
   1) the queen carrying some of the old fungus from her old home.
   2) the fungus and the ant colony needing each other.
   3) the ants feeding the fungus chewed-up leaves.
   4) the fungus being adapted to growing in ant gardens.
   5) the close relationship of these organisms.

3. ① ② ③ ④ ⑤

4. Trichonympha have adapted to life in a termite's digestive tract. Which of the following best describes this situation?
   1) This is an example of long-term adaptation.
   2) It is an example of short-term adaptation.
   3) Only termites can benefit from the partnership.
   4) Trichonympha are dangerous bacteria.
   5) Trichonympha are a lot like lichens.

4. ① ② ③ ④ ⑤

5. You could infer from this passage that
   1) these are the only examples of cooperation in nature.
   2) these are representative examples of co-operation.
   3) everything in nature competes.
   4) the organisms mentioned must be pretty smart to have figured out how to do this.
   5) termites consciously decided to keep bacteria in their digestive tracts.

5. ① ② ③ ④ ⑤

Subject Matter Review (continued)

6. What detail best supports the statement, "This ant-fungus association is extremely close. Neither could get along without the other"?
   1) Certain species of ants grow fungus gardens.
   2) This fungus grows only in ant gardens.
   3) The ants have special adaptations for fungus farming.
   4) Fungus prefer to live in ant gardens.
   5) There isn't sufficient information to answer this question.

6. ① ② ③ ④ ⑤

Answers:

1. 5	2. 2	3. 1
4. 1	5. 2	6. 2

CHECK YOUR ANSWERS

Dr. Lewis Thomas, well-known biologist, selected "Seven True Wonders of the World" for *Reader's Digest*. Below is his "Number 3 Wonder." Read the passage and answer the questions.

PRACTICE THE SKILLS

My number three wonder is *oncideres*, a species of beetle encountered by a pathologist friend of mine who lives in Houston and has a lot of mimosa trees in his backyard. This beetle is not new, but it qualifies as a Modern Wonder because of the exceedingly modern questions raised for evolutionary biologists about the three consecutive things on the mind of the female of the species. Her first thought is for a mimosa tree, which she finds and climbs, ignoring all other kinds of trees in the vicinity. Her second thought is for the laying of eggs, which she does by crawling out on a limb, cutting a longitudinal slit with her mandible and depositing her eggs beneath the slit. Her third and last thought concerns the welfare of her offspring; beetle larvae cannot survive in live wood, so she backs up a foot or so and cuts a neat girdle all around the limb, through the bark and down into the cambium. It takes her eight hours to finish this cabinetwork. Then she leaves and where she goes I do not know. The limb dies from the girdling, falls to the ground in the next breeze, the larvae feed and grow into the next generation, and the questions lie there unanswered.... Does this smart beetle know what she is doing? And how did the mimosa tree enter the picture in its evolution? Left to themselves, unpruned, mimosa trees have a life expectancy of twenty-five to thirty years. **Pruned each year, which is what the beetle's girdling labor accomplishes, the tree can flourish for a century. The mimosa-beetle relationship is an elegant example of symbiotic partnership, a phenomenon now recognized as pervasive in nature. It is good for us to have around on our intellectual mantelpiece such creatures as this insect and its friend the tree, tor they keep reminding us how little we know about nature.**

Now answer these questions.

1. Dr. Thomas says this is a *symbiotic* partner-   1. ① ② ③ ④ ⑤
   ship in which both organisms benefit. Which
   of the following explains this statement?
   1) The beetle uses a branch of the tree to
      hatch its eggs but the tree isn't ad-
      versely affected.
   2) The mimosa encourages the beetle to lay
      its eggs in a branch.
   3) Beetle eggs can only mature in dead mi-
      mosa branches, so the beetle prunes the
      tree.
   4) The eggs need to hatch on the ground, so
      the limb falls off.
   5) The tree profits because pruning makes it
      live longer; the beetle benefits by hav-
      ing a place to lay its eggs.

2. Which of the following best tells the main   2. ① ② ③ ④ ⑤
   idea of this selection?
   1) A partnership can exist between a tree
      and a beetle.
   2) Partnerships in nature are always like
      this one.
   3) It tells how much we know about nature.
   4) It's all about symbiotic relationships.
   5) Relationships always benefit both organ-
      isms.

Subject Matter Review (continued)

3. The thing that puzzles Dr. Thomas the most is   3. ① ② ③ ④ ⑤
   1) how we were able to find out about this relationship.
   2) why mimosa trees need to be pruned.
   3) how the beetle knows how to do the same things in the same order from generation to generation.
   4) why beetle larvae can't live in living wood.
   5) why the beetle doesn't prune oak trees.

4. Dr. Thomas is one of our most brilliant scientists, yet he implies   4. ① ② ③ ④ ⑤
   1) evolutionary biologists completely understand this partnership.
   2) beetles are capable of thought much like human beings.
   3) mimosa need beetles, but beetles don't need mimosa.
   4) we really don't know very much about nature.
   5) beetles couldn't live without mimosa trees.

Answers:
1. 5   2. 1   3. 3   4. 4

CHECK YOUR
ANSWERS

Subject Matter Review (continued)

Much of our language is borrowed from Latin and Greek. This is especially true of words used in science. You have a better chance of unlocking science words if you know a little about Greek and Latin words. It isn't necessary to study these languages to know many of these scientific words because the same parts make up many of the words you use every day.

For instance, <u>biology</u> is a word formed of two parts. <u>Bio-</u> means "life" and <u>-logy</u> means "to study"—so <u>biology</u> means "the study of life."

Below is a chart of some common scientific words. Fill in the blanks on the right of the chart with the meanings we associate with these words.

LEARN THE SKILLS

	LITERAL MEANING	PRACTICAL MEANING
bio+logy	life+study	_____
photo+synthesis (synthetic)	light+manufacture	_____
geo+graphy (graph, graphic)	earth+picture	_____
thermo+meter (metry, metric)	heat+measure	_____
tele+scope (scopic)	far+to see	_____
micro+be	small+being (life)	_____

Now make your own chart like the one above with these words: *microscope, thermosynthesis, photography, geography, micrometer, geology, biosynthesis, thermography.*

	LITERAL MEANING	PRACTICAL MEANING
_____	_____	_____
_____	_____	_____
_____	_____	_____
_____	_____	_____
_____	_____	_____
_____	_____	_____
_____	_____	_____
_____	_____	_____

Subject Matter Review (continued)

Answers:
PRACTICAL MEANINGS: *Biology* is the study of life. *Photosynthesis* is the way plants make food with light. *Geography* is the study of earth forms. *Thermometer* is an instrument to measure heat. A *telescope* is an instrument used to see things that are far away. *Microbes* are small living things.

CHECK YOUR ANSWERS

YOUR CHART:

	LITERAL MEANING	PRACTICAL MEANING
micro+scope	small+to see	an instrument for seeing small things
thermo+synthesis	heat+to make	to produce by means of heat
photo+graphy	light+picture	to make a picture with light
geo+metry	earth+measure	a branch of mathematics
micro+meter	small+to measure	an instrument to measure tiny things
geo+logy	earth+to study	study of the earth
bio+synthesis	life+to make	to produce by biological means
thermo+graphy	heat+picture	pictures made with heat

Here are some more short reading selections dealing with science material. Read the passages and answer the questions.

PRACTICE THE SKILLS

Symbiosis (sim-bee-OH-sis), the phenomenon in nature which refers to the many ways organisms live together, is the rule in nature rather than the exception. Cooperation in nature is far more common than competition. In fact, most examples of competition have the net effect of cooperation.

1. <u>Symbiosis</u> means "living together." Which of the following is the best description of its derivation?
   1) sym=together, bio=life, osis=condition
   2) sym=together, bi=two, oosis=eggs
   3) sym=life, bi=two, oosis=eggs
   4) symb=sound, ioo=together, sis=condition
   5) symbi=noise, osis=condition

1. ① ② ③ ④ ⑤

2. What does the word <u>symphony</u> mean?
   1) an orchestra
   2) a kind of music
   3) to put sounds together
   4) to make noise
   5) none of the above

2. ① ② ③ ④ ⑤

All crabs have wrinkles on the undersides of their bodies. Superstitious Japanese fishermen saw pictures in these convolutions. Some of them reminded the fishermen of an ancient warlord. Those crabs that looked the most like the famous ancestor were returned to the sea unharmed.

Today, after generations of fishermen and more generations of crabs, many crabs in the warm currents surrounding Japan carry on their stomachs a remarkable likeness of this ancient Japanese warrior.

3. The word <u>convolution</u> means   3. ① ② ③ ④ ⑤
   1) crabs
   2) stomachs
   3) wrinkles
   4) warlords
   5) pictures

4. This article is mainly about   4. ① ② ③ ④ ⑤
   1) the fishing industry in Japan
   2) likenesses of warlords
   3) the wrinkles on crabs
   4) Japanese folklore
   5) how natural selection is affected by man

5. Which of these stories from the video is   5. ① ② ③ ④ ⑤
   similar to this one?
   1) the way DDT accumulates at various levels
      of the food web
   2) the story of the peppered moth
   3) the extinction of the dinosaurs
   4) the succession of living things on Earth
   5) the lynx, rabbit, caribou example

One of the most remarkable creations is the Portugese man-of-war. It is a relative of the jellyfishes and floats around warm ocean currents, blown from place to place by the capricious tropical winds.

Incredibly, the portugese man-of-war isn't one animal. It is technically a colony of highly specialized organisms living in such close union that it is impossible to distinguish one from the other.

6. What does the word <u>capricious</u> mean?   6. ① ② ③ ④ ⑤
   1) unpredictable
   2) warm
   3) harsh
   4) bitter
   5) southern

**Subject
Matter
Review**
(continued)

7. Which of the quotes from the video best applies to this reading selection?   7. ① ② ③ ④ ⑤
   1) The diversity of life on Earth is rich beyond understanding.
   2) Biologists have so far discovered one and a half million species of plants.
   3) And even for humans, most environmental problems are pretty complex.
   4) Mutations are the result of changes in the genetic code of an organism.
   5) Animals and plants adapt to the seasons by taking advantage of good weather and avoiding the bad.

Answers:

1. 1	2. 3	3. 3	4. 5
5. 2	6. 1	7. 1	

**CHECK YOUR
ANSWERS**

Just for Fun

World's Easiest Biology Quiz

1. What is the color of black eyed Susans' eyes?
2. To what family of plants do Jerusalem artichokes belong, and where do they come from?
3. For what creatures were the Canary Islands named?
4. What color are purple finches?
5. When you hear "the voice of the turtle," what does it sound like?
6. What's the difference between a buffalo and a bison?

Answers:

1. chocolate brown
2. They're not artichokes, and they aren't from Jerusalem. They are native American sunflowers.
3. Dogs. Canary is Latin for the same word canine comes from.
4. crimson or pink
5. "Coooo. This Bible reference is talking about "turtle doves."
6. A buffalo is a cow or ox-like animal. A bison is what an Australian washes his hands in. ("basin"—Sorry.)

**CHECK YOUR
ANSWERS**

Test-Taking Tip

It is impossible for us to teach you the exact questions you'll find on a test. This is why we are working so hard to help you improve your reading skills so you can figure out the answers for yourself.

Sometimes questions test the information you already know, but usually the answers you are looking for will be in the reading selections.

Some people read the test questions before they read the passage. This helps them zero in on details they need to answer the questions correctly.

The extra practice for this chapter is arranged with the questions first so you can practice this technique.

In this practice section, read the questions first, then read the reading selection, and then answer the questions.

EXTRA PRACTICE

1. According to the article, ecology means
   1) living together
   2) symbiosis
   3) the study of cycles in nature
   4) the study of homes
   5) classification of living arrangements

1. ① ② ③ ④ ⑤

2. Symbiosis means
   1) living together
   2) the same as ecology
   3) scavenging
   4) predation
   5) all of the above

2. ① ② ③ ④ ⑤

3. Which of the following is not an example of scavenging?
   1) seagulls gathering on the beach where you just had a picnic
   2) beetles which lay their eggs in a mimosa tree branch
   3) hyenas eating an antelope carcass that lions have killed
   4) pigeons eating the corn spilled on a country road
   5) fruit flies on spoiled apples

3. ① ② ③ ④ ⑤

4. This article implies that natural relationships are   4. ① ② ③ ④ ⑤
   1) extremely violent
   2) not violent at all
   3) not always in balance
   4) always in balance
   5) mostly cooperative

Ecology, the study of natural cycles, is a fascinating look at the intricacies of nature. Everything fits into three general classifications of living arrangements. The first is called *symbiosis*, which means two types of organisms live together in a mutually beneficial relationship.

Scavenging is another category. Scavengers are organisms in charge of cleaning up. They are the janitors of nature.

The third class is predation. Organisms that prey on other organisms are known as *predators*.

Sometimes it is difficult to distinguish between these functions of nature. Generally speaking, in the world of nature, there is more symbiosis than there is scavenging, and there is more scavenging than there is predation.

(Now go back and answer the questions about this passage.)

Answers:
   1. 3   2. 1   3. 2   4. 5

**CHECK YOUR
ANSWERS**

Chapter
Seven
Science

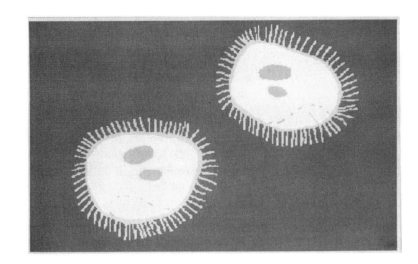

Today's lesson will challenge your concentration as well as your ability to apply the skills you've been learning. The big thing is the vocabulary. If you follow these exercises, you should have an increased ability to unlock the hidden meanings in scientific material.

This program introduces you to the most basic unit of life: the cell. The video takes you into its inner workings.

Of great importance is the manner in which cells reproduce. You'll learn about two types of reproduction—

how they are similar and how they differ.

Next, the program takes up the subject of how life codes are transferred from one generation to the next. Knowledge in this field of biology has grown dramatically over the past few years.

These basic ideas are then expanded to show you how scientists apply their knowledge to the system of classifying living things.

Goal-Setting Exercise for Program 7

Unless you just happen to have an electron microscope stashed away in the playroom, you're not likely ever to see most of the things discussed in this lesson.

You can, however, get an idea of the nature of a cell by observing the yolk of an egg. (Just the yolk, now.)

An egg yolk is said, by many scientists, to be the largest cell. If you very carefully lift the yolk free from the white, you'll find that it does indeed have its own cell membrane.

Egg yolks try to take on the shape of the container into which they are placed. This is another cell-like feature.

Yolks are three-dimensional. They have length, height, and width. When you see pictures of cells in a book, it's easy to think of them as being flat, without thickness. Remember, cells have thickness, too.

The membrane around the yolk is semipermeable (sem-ee-PURM-ee-uh-buhl). This means some things can pass through it and some things can't. It's selective. Nutrients can get in; waste can get out.

As in cells, the material inside a yolk is a colloid. Colloids are mixtures which hold in suspension those particles too large to pass through a membrane.

Now answer these questions.

1. Which of the following tells what this article is mainly about?
   1) egg yolks
   2) the way cells are
   3) cells and eggs
   4) the way cells and egg yolks are alike
   5) the way cells and egg yolks are different

1. ① ② ③ ④ ⑤

2. Which of the following is *not* listed as a similarity?
   1) Yolks and cells reproduce themselves.
   2) Both are three-dimensional.
   3) The material in both is called a colloid.
   4) Cells and egg yolks are surrounded by membranes.
   5) There isn't sufficient information to answer this question.

2. ① ② ③ ④ ⑤

Goal-
Setting
Exercise
for
Program 7
(continued)

3. What is the *implied* major difference between   3. ① ② ③ ④ ⑤
   cells and egg yolks?
   1) color
   2) size
   3) shape
   4) structure
   5) contents

4. <u>Semi-permeable</u> means a membrane that   4. ① ② ③ ④ ⑤
   1) is selective
   2) has large particles
   3) is tiny
   4) 2) but not 1)
   5) 2) and 3) but not 1)

5. The style in which this article is written is   5. ① ② ③ ④ ⑤
   1) scientific
   2) formal
   3) colloquial
   4) informal
   5) satirical

6. You can infer from this article that   6. ① ② ③ ④ ⑤
   1) transfer of nutrients depends on the size
       of the particles.
   2) cell cytoplasm is homologous to the white
       of an egg.
   3) plant cells are more like egg yolks than
       animal cells are.
   4) all cells look exactly like an egg yolk.
   5) There isn't enough information to answer
       this question.

Answers for Goal-Setting Exercises:
   1. 4   2. 1   3. 2
   4. 1   5. 4   6. 1

CHECK YOUR
ANSWERS

Viewing Prescription for Program 7

❏ If you got them **all right** …

You're doing a super job!

❏ If you missed number **1** …

You may still be having some trouble identifying the *main idea*. Part of this program is devoted to finding the main idea in scientific readings.

❏ If you missed number **2** …

Try to find *details* in the program.

❏ If you missed number **3** …

The program has many examples in which you will need to *compare and contrast* ideas. Be alert to these examples.

❏ If you missed number **4** …

This is a *context* question. This is a very important skill when reading science material. Review what is said about context in Chapter One before you watch program 7.

❏ If you missed number **5** …

This is a question of *style*. Review what you have learned about it. Be alert to the variety of styles used in this lesson.

❏ If you missed number **6** …

Watch carefully for *implied meanings* in the program. Also pay particular attention to the Test-Taking Tip in this chapter.

Vocabulary for Program 7

The words connected with this program are commonly used in the field of biology. Try to become familiar with some of them before you watch the show.

LEARN THE SKILLS

chromosome (KROM-oh-soam) The chromosomes contain the "program" that determines cell development.

excrete (ek-SKREET) means to give off waste.

unicellular (you-nuh-SELL-you-lar) means an organism with only one cell.

multi-cellular (mul-tee-SELL-you-lar) means an organism with many cells. All plants and animals you can see without a microscope are multi-cellular.

taxonomy (tax-AH-no-mee) is a list in order of the simplest to the most complex.

colloid (KAH-loyd) is a mixture in which large particles are suspended. Gelatin dessert is an example of a colloid. The material in a cell is in "colloidal (kah-LOYD-uhl) suspension."

cell (SELL) is the basic unit of life. It is the smallest unit that can stand by itself and be said to be "alive."

organelle (or-gun-ELL) means literally "little organ." This is the name given to all the little parts of a cell.

DNA is the abbreviation for Deoxyri-boNucleic Acid. This complex chemical compound determines characteristics passed on from generation to generation.

nucleus (NEW-klee-us) is the cell part that is the center for life.

cytoplasm (SIGH-toh-plaz-uhm) is the jelly-like material in cells. All the other cell parts are scattered through the cytoplasm.

chlorophyll (KLOR-uh-fill) is the green material in plants.

mitosis (my-TOH-sis) The process in which two cells each contribute genetic information to create a new cell.

hypothesis (high-PAH-thuh-sis) is a working idea or a guess about the answer to a scientific question.

genus (GEE-nuss) means general type, and is one part of the classification of living things.

species (SPEE-sees) refers to related organisms. Organisms are commonly called by their genus and species. Humans are of the genus *homo* and the species *sapiens*.

Now
Watch
Program
7

1. The functions of life were either mentioned or implied in several places in the program. Here is a list of them:

   … Nutrition   … Digestion   … Respiration

   … Excretion   … Secretion   … Response

   … Biosynthesis   … Reproduction

2. Photosynthesis, the way plants make food from the sun, is the most important biological process since it sustains all other life (except for one extremely rare exception).

3. Cells reproduce in two ways. In *mitosis*, cells split to produce another cell exactly like the original. In *meiosis*, characteristics of two cells are joined to form a new cell.

4. Cells of your body reproduce by mitosis.

5. Germ cells, the ones that create another human being, reproduce through meiosis.

6. Gregor Mendel made the first discoveries leading to the study of genetics by observing pea plants.

7. We now know that the code that determines what an organism will be is in the complicated chemistry of DNA.

8. Biologists have organized all life in a taxonomy of Kingdom, Phylum, Class, Order, Family, Genus, and Species. The accepted kingdoms are animal, plant, fungus, protist, and monera.

9. An organism is commonly referred to by its genus and species.

10. Only one species of humans is alive on Earth at this time.

**LEARN THE
FACTS**

We've mentioned that the vocabulary of this lesson is tough. Don't be afraid of it, though. This next passage will help translate the language into everyday terms.

Read about "Cell Pie" and complete the accompanying exercises.

**PRACTICE
THE SKILLS**

CELL PIE

Ingredients:
1	golf ball
2	small sausages
2-3	feet of Christmas ribbon
2	gumdrops
1	cubic inch of cellulose sponge
1	package of gelatin dessert

Line a 10-inch pie tin with enough plastic sandwich wrap to extend slightly over the sides of the tin.

Place the golf ball near the center of the pie tin. Place the two sausages about 3 inches from the golf ball on either side of it. Their natural arc should match the curve of the golf ball.

Now fold the ribbon in a serpentine (snakelike) pattern about 4 inches long. Fold it back and forth so it will stand on edge. Throw in the sponge (no pun intended) about four inches from the golf ball.

The gumdrops come next. Just put them in the pan wherever you feel like it.

Now, prepare the gelatin in the usual way and fill the pie tin with the dessert. Allow to cool and set.

You can use the sandwich wrap to lift the "cell" out of the pie tin.

If you ever decided to make this "cell pie," you'd have a fairly accurate model of a cell. The cell pie is about *10 billion* (1×10^{10} power) times the size and weight of a human liver cell.

By the way, this is the recipe for an animal cell. If you want a plant cell, leave out the gumdrops, put in a ping-pong ball and two or three green jelly beans, and leave the whole mess in the pie tin.

Now answer these questions.

1. The author's main purpose in writing this passage is to
   1) have everyone make a model of a cell.
   2) use everyday items to show the relationships of cell parts.
   3) make you smile.
   4) introduce the complexity of cell structure.
   5) none of the above

1. ① ② ③ ④ ⑤

2. Which of the following is the best example of a scientific detail in this article?
   1) Use a 10-inch pie tin.
   2) It's a fairly accurate model.
   3) The cell pie is about 10 billion times the size and weight of a human liver cell.
   4) Plant cells have green jelly beans in them.
   5) Leave the whole mess in the pie tin.

2. ① ② ③ ④ ⑤

Subject
Matter
Review
(continued)

3. The article says, "Throw in the sponge (no pun intended)." A pun is a joke based on words that have double meanings. "Throw in the sponge" means
   1) clean up your act
   2) take advantage
   3) escape
   4) run away
   5) quit

3. ① ② ③ ④ ⑤

4. It is implied that
   1) animal cells have some parts that plant cells do not.
   2) plant cells have some parts that animal cells do not.
   3) cells are made up of tiny parts.
   4) neither 1) nor 2)
   5) 1), 2), and 3)

4. ① ② ③ ④ ⑤

5. Why does the article specify green jelly beans?
   1) They represent the green parts of the plants.
   2) Just for effect. They could be any color.
   3) Green jelly beans are the easiest to find.
   4) They're the right size.
   5) 1) and 3)

5. ① ② ③ ④ ⑤

Now read this.

   Biologists make a distinction between the terms *analogous* and *homologous*. *Analogous* means "for the same function." *Homologous* means "the same kind of structure." Organs can be compared as analogous, homologous, or a combination.

Using these definitions, classify the following comparisons.   6. ① ② ③ ④ ⑤

6. Which of the following pairs are analogous?
    1)   the wings of a bird and the wings of a mosquito
    2)   the trunk of an elephant and the hands of a monkey
    3)   the wings of a bat and the hands of a human
    4)   the flipper of a whale and the arms of a human
    5)   1) and 2) but not 3) and 4)

7. Which of the following pairs are homologous?   7. ① ② ③ ④ ⑤
    1)   the wings of a bird and the wings of a mosquito
    2)   the trunk of an elephant and the hands of a monkey
    3)   the wings of a bat and the hands of a human
    4)   the flipper of a whale and the arms of a human
    5)   3) and 4) but not 1) and 2)

8. Which of the following are *not* both analogous   8. ① ② ③ ④ ⑤
   and homologous?
    1)   the hands of a monkey and the hands of a human
    2)   the flippers of a whale and the fins of a fish
    3)   the feathers of a bird and the scales of a reptile
    4)   the toenails of a human and the hooves of a horse
    5)   an elephant's trunk and a pig's snout

9. What is the best title for this passage?   9. ① ② ③ ④ ⑤
    1)   Wings
    2)   Two Different Meanings
    3)   Big Words in Biology
    4)   Analogous and Homologous Explained
    5)   Worthwhile Information

10. The pie tin that holds "cell pie" is   10. ① ② ③ ④ ⑤
    1) analogous to a cell wall
    2) homologous to a cell wall
    3) analogous and representative
    4) representative only
    5) none of the above

Use the chart to answer questions 11 and 12.

INGREDIENT	REPRESENTS	BECAUSE
Sandwich Wrap	Cell Membrane (MEM-brain) is the skin of the cell.	It holds the mixture.
Golf Ball	Nucleus (NEW-klee-us) is the most important organelle.	It has the shape and its own covering.
Golf Ball Core	Nucleolus (new-klee-OH-lus) literally means "little nucleus." It's an organelle found inside the nucleus.	It's inside the golf ball, or nucleus.
Golf Ball Rubber Windings	Chromatin (KROAM-uh-tin) is the part of the nucleus of a cell that contains the chromosomes. Chromatin comes from a word which means color. It's the coloring in the cells.	It resembles the long chromosome strands.
Sausages	Mitochondria (my-tuh-KON-dree-uh) is the plural of the word mitochondrion, which is the organelle in charge of respiration in the cell.	They resemble mitochondria and both are full of fat and protein.
Ribbon	Endoplasmic Reticulum (en-doh-PLAZ-mik ree-TICK-you-lum) is the ribbon-like organelle in the cell. It moves nutrients around the cell.	An endoplasmic reticulum looks like a ribbon winding through the cell body.
Sponge	Golgi Apparatus (GOAL-gee) is another complex organelle. Its job is to transport cell products outside the cell.	The Golgi soaks up cell products much like a sponge would soak up spilled milk.
Gumdrops	Lysosomes (LIE-so-soamz) are the enzyme factories. They are also responsible for dissolving dead cells.	Gumdrops are concentrated energy bits and so are lysosomes.
Gelatin Dessert	Cytoplasm (SIGH-toe-plaz-um) is the living stuff in the cell that does not include the organelles. Cyto- is a prefix which refers to cells. Anytime you see a word with "cyto" in it, you know it's about cells.	Cytoplasm is a colloid—so is gelatin dessert.

PLANT DIFFERENCES

Ping Pong Ball	Vacuole (VAK-you-ohl) is the organelle that is a storage place for food and water.	Vacuoles appear to be vacant spaces in the cells.
Green Jelly Beans	Chloroplastids (KLOR-oh-plas-tidz) are the green organelles in plants.	They are the right color and they are food.
Pie Tin	Cell Walls in plants have an additional layer of "skin." It's what makes fruit crunchy.	Pie tins are rigid; so are plant cell walls.

11. According to the chart, the core of the golf   11. ① ② ③ ④ ⑤
    ball represents
    1) nucleus
    2) cytoplasm
    3) nucleolus
    4) mitochondria
    5) chromatin

12. Which of the organelles delivers cell prod-   12. ① ② ③ ④ ⑤
    ucts to the other cells?
    1) endoplasmic reticulum
    2) Golgi apparatus
    3) chromatin
    4) lysosomes
    5) mitochondria

Answers:

   1. 2   2. 3   3. 5   4. 5   5. 1
   6. 1   7. 5   8. 2   9. 4
   10. 3—The pie tin is analogous and representative. It holds the cell pie together, so it
       serves the same purpose as the cell wall.
   11. 3   12. 2

CHECK YOUR
ANSWERS

Subject Matter Review (continued)

Skill Helper

Here is a list of 10 everyday words which are related in some way to words used in this lesson. Be alert to the familiar parts of unfamiliar words.

                                                    is related to:

1. Geneology   _____
2. Unicycle   _____
3. Multitude   _____
4. Kodachrome   _____
5. Generic   _____
6. Excavate   _____
7. Multimedia   _____
8. Universe   _____
9. Blood Plasma   _____
10. Nuclear Power   _____

Answers:

1. GENeology/GENUS
3. MULTItude/MULTIcellular
5. GENeric/GENus
7. MULTImedia/MULTIcellular
9. Blood PLASMa/cytoPLASM

2. UNIcycle/UNIcellular
4. KodaCHROME/CHROMosome
6. EXcavate/EXcrete
8. UNIverse/UNIcellular
10. NUCLEar power/NUCLEus

CHECK YOUR ANSWERS

Just for Fun

We can't swear this story is true, but it's told widely enough to make you wonder.

When European scientists first visited Australia, they were overwhelmed by the unusual animal life. One of them asked a native the name of the strange, long-tailed animal that hopped all over the place.

The aborigine answered: "Kangaroo."

Supposedly, that's how that animal was named.

Years later, people studying the native language learned that the word kangaroo means, roughly: "I don't know, either."

Test-Taking Tip

Test designers don't intentionally write "trick" questions. However, in order to make the choices really test the skill they are after, they must think of "reasonably wrong" answers. Before you answer a question, be sure your answer is really right. Example:

> **Fertilized egg cells develop exponentially; that is, as they divide, one cell becomes two, two cells become four, and so forth. After six such divisions, how many cells are there?**
>   1) 6
>   2) 12
>   3) 32
> *   4) 64
>   5) 128

Answer 4 is correct because the passage implies that all the cells double each time they divide. One doubled six times equals 64. The other answers are wrong, although they sound reasonable.

Read this short passage and answer the questions.

EXTRA PRACTICE

> **Mendel's hypotheses about breeding were the result of many experiments, careful record keeping, and mathematical evaluation. This doesn't mean they're true. It merely means they're the simplest explanations, based on the facts as observed by Mendel and thousands of scientists since.**
>
> **You can say these hypotheses are reasonable or logical, but those terms are difficult to measure and sometimes colored by opinion. The whole study of genetics is based on what scientists *believe* is true.**
>
> **Most people think emotions are not a part of science. The real value of a hypothesis is that it enables scientists to predict facts. This takes imagination, which is little more than emotional guesswork.**

Now answer these questions.

1. This passage implies that science
    1) is a matter of well established facts.
    2) is totally a result of experimentation.
    3) has to do with the way scientists feel about something.
    4) is completely objective.
    5) is free of emotions.

1. ① ② ③ ④ ⑤

2. This passage implies that Mendel   2. ① ② ③ ④ ⑤
   1) was methodical.
   2) was right in his assumptions.
   3) learned all there was to know about ge-
      netics.
   4) found the only solution.
   5) 3) and 4) only

3. Which of the following is *not* necessary for a   3. ① ② ③ ④ ⑤
   good hypothesis?
   1) Other people must get the same results
      when they follow the experiments.
   2) It must be true.
   3) It should inspire people to look more
      deeply into the subject.
   4) It must be based entirely on facts.
   5) It must not have an error in it.

Answers:
  1. 3   2. 1   3. 2

CHECK YOUR
ANSWERS

Chapter
Eight
Science

People have tried to understand the nature of the Earth since the beginning of time. Humans have looked for answers in the folklore, superstitions, religion, and science of every culture. Earth science uses information from many other sciences.

The more we study it, the more we realize that we still know very little about the Earth; and our ideas change every time we learn something new.

The big idea is that we live in a world of constant change. Tiny events in one part of the world can create major changes elsewhere.

Despite the massive energy and wondrous workings of the Earth, the video suggests a fragile nature to it all. The balance is so delicate that even small disturbances could destroy the entire system.

Goal-Setting Exercise for Program 8

Read these short passages and answer the questions.

Fossils of ancient aquatic plants and animals are often found in exposed sections of sedimentary rock layers on mountain sides far from and much higher than the sea.

1. Which of the following is not a question suggested by this passage?
   1) How did the plants and animals get in the rock?
   2) What happened to the sea?
   3) How many were there?
   4) Why are they in sedimentary rock?
   5) What happened to expose the rocks?

   1. ① ② ③ ④ ⑤

2. You could infer all of the following except
   1) oceans once covered the spot where the fossils are.
   2) fossils were lifted to their present position.
   3) oceans were once deep enough to cover all the mountains on Earth.
   4) water plays an important role in the formation of sedimentary rock.
   5) something happened to turn the animals to stone.

   2. ① ② ③ ④ ⑤

Goal-
Setting
Exercise
for
Program 8
(continued)

Some styrofoam pellets about an eighth of an inch in diameter and a handful each of lead BBs and gravel were placed in a container and mixed uniformly. The container was placed on a table that vibrated constantly.

3. After a time, you observe
   1) the mixture becomes more uniform through-out.
   2) the BBs find their way to the top, the stones seek the middle, and the styrofoam sinks to the bottom.
   3) styrofoam, being lighter, rises to the top; the stones tend to be in the middle.
   4) the mixture would stay just as it was when it was placed in the container.
   5) 1) and 4) but not 2) or 3)

3. ① ② ③ ④ ⑤

The density of the crust of the Earth is $2^{1}/2$ to $3^{1}/3$ times the density of water. The innermost core of the Earth is 10 to 17 times as heavy as water.

4. The mantle, the layer of the Earth just under the crust, is
   1) less dense than the crust.
   2) less dense than water.
   3) 12 times the density of water.
   4) more dense than the inner core.
   5) more dense than the crust.

4. ① ② ③ ④ ⑤

5. The BB/gravel/styrofoam example
   1) shows how solids can "float" on one an-other.
   2) is a model which demonstrates the layers of the Earth.
   3) demonstrates the effect of earthquakes.
   4) neither 1) nor 2)
   5) both 1) and 2) but not 3)

5. ① ② ③ ④ ⑤

Goal-Setting Exercise for Program 8 (continued)

Rain falling on the land dissolves minerals as it runs through the ground and into the rivers. Water in rivers drains into the oceans, where the water is evaporated, causing rain and starting the process over again.

6. The best title for this paragraph is
   1) The Water Cycle
   2) Oceans and Rivers
   3) Rivers and Rain
   4) Minerals and Rivers
   5) Rivers and Evaporation

6.① ② ③ ④ ⑤

7. Only the water is evaporated; impurities are not. Which of the following is *not* a result of this principle?
   1) The oceans become more mineral-laden all the time.
   2) A teakettle "limes up" on the inside.
   3) Distilled water has no minerals in it.
   4) Water is the universal solvent.
   5) Rainwater has fewer minerals in it than does well water.

7.① ② ③ ④ ⑤

Answers for Goal-Setting Exercise:

1. 3	2. 3	3. 3	4. 5
5. 5	6. 1	7. 4	

CHECK YOUR ANSWERS

Viewing Prescription for Program 8

❏ If you got them **all right** …

you're ready for the big time! All of these questions are based on the inference skills. If you had a great deal of difficulty with these questions, go back and review the suggested pages before you watch the program.

❏ If you missed number **1** or **2** …

review chapter 2 in the workbook.

❏ If you missed number **3** …

review chapter 4 in the workbook.

❏ If you missed number **4** or **5** …

these questions refer to using information from one situation and applying it in another setting. We'll give you more help in this lesson.

❏ If you missed number **6** …

this is a problem of *inferring the main idea*. Review chapter 2 in the workbook.

❏ If you missed number **7** …

review the "Flags" for *cause and effect* on pages 37-39.

Vocabulary for Program 8

Below are some of the "science" words used in the video. Listen for how these words are used in the television program. We'll have some exercises about them later.

LEARN THE WORDS

seismology (size-MAH-low-gee) is the science that studies the vibrations in the Earth caused by earthquakes or other disturbances. Seismographic (size-mo-GRAF-ick) refers to making pictures of ground tremors.

oceanography (oh-shun-AH-gruh-fee) is the study of oceans. The word literally means "ocean pictures."

geography (gee-AH-gruh-fee) is the study of Earth forms.

Vocabulary for Program 8 (continued)

meteorology (me-tee-or-AH-lowğee) is the study of weather and weather patterns.

mantle (MAN-tuhl) refers to the covering of the Earth.

silicon (SILL-uh-kon) is the second most abundant element on Earth. (Oxygen is first.) It makes up a major portion of the mantle.

isotopes (EY-so-toaps) are different forms of the same element.

convection (kuhn-VECK-shun) describes circulating currents in fluids which are caused by differences in temperature.

Pangaea (pan-GEE-uh) refers to a time when all the "land" on Earth was in one piece.

tectonics (teck-TAHN-iks) is the study of the folding and faulting of the Earth's surface.

sedimentary (said-uh-MEN-tuh-ree) is a kind of rock formed by the settling out of minerals in water.

metamorphic (met-uh-MOR-fick) refers to rock that has been "changed" in its structure—usually by heat and pressure.

magma (MAG-muh) is the "liquid" portion of the center of the Earth.

NOW
WATCH
PROGRAM
8

**Subject
Matter
Review**

Subject Matter Review

1. Earth isn't as solid or as unchanging as we tend to believe.
2. Earth's center is only 4,000 miles away from us, but we know very little about it.
3. The core of Earth is mainly iron.
4. Earth's mantle is made up primarily of silicon.
5. The plates of the crust move extremely slowly (by human time scale) about the surface. This motion can be detected by what is called "continental drift."
6. Over two-thirds of the surface of our planet is covered by water.
7. As massive as the cycles of the Earth are, they can be interrupted by human activity.
8. A major reason for space exploration is to learn more about the Earth.

**LEARN THE
FACTS**

Finding Context Clues

Your ability to use context clues depends, in part, on how quickly you can see familiar parts in unfamiliar words.

Below is a list of words used in the video. Make a list of common words which use the capitalized parts.

Example:
    SUBduct—subway, submarine, subterranean, subculture
    subDUCT—tear duct, heat duct, conduct (etc.)

Now make your own list.

radioACTIVE   _____

reJECTed   _____

TRANSform   _____

Notice how the word-mates still have some of the same meaning as the original words.

**LEARN THE
SKILLS**

Inference Patterns

The farther we go in this series, the more difficult the inferences become. The

relationships become less obvious and rely more on qualifying words such as
"all," "some" or "some of the time," "most," or "most of the time."

When you make an inference or draw a conclusion from inferred information, you are trying to do one or more of these things:

■ MAKE A GENERALIZATION

Example: Rocks are heavier than feathers

■ DETERMINE CAUSE AND EFFECT

Example: The wind blew the feathers away, but the rocks are still here.

■ ANTICIPATE AN OUTCOME

Example: If I piled the feathers up again and the wind blew again, what
would happen?

■ SEE AN ANALOGY

Example: Rocks are to feathers as …

… bricks are to dandelion seeds

… beer bottles are to styrofoam cups

… gravel is to dust

Keep these patterns in mind as you complete this lesson.

PRACTICE
THE SKILLS

"Harvey, you're crazy! You expect me to believe that the Earth is
a better ball than that moldy old golf ball?" said Big Jim Dutton.

John and Barry seated themselves at a slanting, wobbling table in
Edna's Cafe, home of fine cooking and free second cup of coffee. The
half dozen "Old Bulls" nearby were already well into their agenda.

John leaned toward Barry. "Big Jim's our president."

"You *elect* a *president*?" Barry asked. He leaned down and placed
a matchbook cover under the short leg of the table.

"No. He just gets here first, so he's the president."

"What do the 'Old Bulls' do?" Barry asked.

"Argue and lie to each other," John said. Edna automatically
picked up the glass coffee pot and headed their way.

Harvey held the ball at arm's length as if observing a fine jewel.
"Suppose you made it the size of the Earth. If you kept the same
proportions, these little dents in the ball would be miles and miles
deep, deeper than any ocean on the Earth. Or, if you made the Earth
as small as this ball, it would be smoother."

"What about the poles, Harvey? The Earth is flat at the poles,"
said Ernie Goodwin.

"Don't care, Ernie. The Earth is only 25 miles flat. It's still
rounder and smoother than this golf ball."

"But Harvey," countered Big Jim, "mountains are miles high.
The Earth can't be smoother. You're a durn fool."

"It's all a matter of scale. The covering on this ball is about the
same thickness as the crust of the Earth, relatively speaking, of
course. Look at this mold. If I rub it off, like this, I've taken more off
this ball than you would take off the Earth if you cut down every
tree. The mold is relatively taller than the trees," said Harvey.

"I've had enough of this relativity junk. Tall mold?" said Big Jim.

"Edna, more coffee." Edna brought more coffee, then some donuts. Ernie offered to borrow a micrometer from the hardware store to prove the point, one way or another, but he didn't. The argument continued.

Now answer these questions.

1. ① ② ③ ④ ⑤

1. From a science point of view, which of the following best tells what this passage is about?
   1) some guys talking about golf balls
   2) breakfast at Edna's
   3) comparing the Earth to a golf ball
   4) the "Old Bulls"
   5) a moldy golf ball

2. ① ② ③ ④ ⑤

2. Which response best tells Harvey's position in the argument?
   1) The Earth is comparatively rough.
   2) If the Earth were as small as the golf ball, it would be smoother.
   3) The Earth is flattened a great deal at the poles.
   4) The mountains are not as high as they seem.
   5) none of the above

3. ① ② ③ ④ ⑤

3. Which of the following is an irrelevant detail?
   1) "The Earth is flattened at the poles by 25 miles."
   2) "It's a matter of scale."
   3) "If you kept the same proportions, those little dents would be miles deep."
   4) "He leaned down and placed a matchbook under the short leg of the table."
   5) "Mold is relatively taller than the trees."

Subject
Matter
Review
(continued)

4. ① ② ③ ④ ⑤

4. Ignoring the discussion about the Earth,
which of the following tells what's going on?
   1) Some friends are visiting over breakfast
      coffee.
   2) It's a description of Edna's Cafe.
   3) It tells you about Harvey.
   4) It's about the comparative smoothness of
      the Earth.
   5) It's about the dimples on a golf ball.

5. ① ② ③ ④ ⑤

5. Again, ignoring the science information,
which of the following best describes the
tone of this selection?
   1) argumentative
   2) formal
   3) ominous
   4) scientific
   5) informal

6. ① ② ③ ④ ⑤

6. Which of the following best defines
"micrometer?"
   1) a measuring device that uses a small
      balance beam
   2) a device for measuring the Earth
   3) something used to measure small objects
   4) a yardstick
   5) none of the above

7. ① ② ③ ④ ⑤

7. You could conclude from this passage that
   1) the men were scientists.
   2) this was the first time at Edna's for
      most.
   3) they'd rather argue than find a solution.
   4) they are angry with one another.
   5) Barry is a regular customer at Edna's.

Answers:
1. 3   2. 2   3. 4   4. 1   5. 5
6. 3—"micro"=small; "meter"=measure
7. 3—Arguing is what the "Old Bulls" do. Ernie offered to solve the problem, but he
   didn't. If they had truly wanted a solution, they'd have measured the ball and
   figured it out.

CHECK YOUR
ANSWERS

Subject
Matter
Review
(continued)

Test-Taking Tip

Below is a list of Test-Taking flags, words that help you decide how to analyze what a particular test term is asking for.

CRITICIZE—asks you to EVALUATE and make JUDGMENTS.

DESCRIBE—wants you to use DETAILS to tell about the MAIN IDEA or other DETAILS.

DISTINGUISH—wants you to COMPARE and CONTRAST, or tell how things are similar and how they are different.

EVALUATE—may mean for you to give your OPINION or make a JUDGMENT based on the information given.

NAME, TELL, LIST, or ENUMERATE—wants you to give DETAILS.

TRACE—wants you to list something in ORDER.

PROVE—asks you to tell WHY something is true.

DEFINE—asks for the meaning of a word or idea.

Below is another account of the "golf ball/Earth" analogy. Once again, however, we've given you the questions first so you can practice the skill of scanning.

Here are three rules to help you become a better "scanner":

- Know what details you want before you start reading.
- When you find a detail you want, read enough on both sides of it to be sure you understand it.
- Ignore all the irrelevant details.

EXTRA
PRACTICE

1. ① ② ③ ④ ⑤

1. Which of the following is the depth of the
   dimples on a golf ball in relation to the
   size of Earth?
   1) $12\frac{1}{2}$
   2) 25 miles
   3) 302 million
   4) 17 miles
   5) none of the above

2. ① ② ③ ④ ⑤

2. Which of the following is the diameter of the
   Earth?
   1) 25 miles
   2) 8,000 miles
   3) 3.02×10^8 miles
   4) 17 miles
   5) none of the above

3. ① ② ③ ④ ⑤

3. Which of the following tells how flat the
   Earth is at the poles?
   1) 3.02×10^8 miles
   2) 17 miles
   3) 8,000 miles
   4) 302 million miles
   5) none of the above

4. ① ② ③ ④ ⑤

4. According to this article, the consistency of
   magma is much like that of
   1) Turkish taffy
   2) water
   3) ice
   4) glass
   5) none of the above

5. ① ② ③ ④ ⑤

5. The continental plates are said to be
   analogous to
   1) Turkish taffy
   2) a golf ball
   3) ice on a river
   4) magma
   5) the bottom of a river

Now read quickly through this passage, trying to pick up just the details
necessary to answer these questions.

Suppose you *could* make a golf ball the size of the Earth and fling
it out in the universe. You'd find the dimpled surface now has dents
in it about 25 miles deep and 120 miles across. The diameter of the
Earth is 302 million (3.02×10^8) times the size of a golf ball, so any
imperfection would be magnified 302 million times. Since the
distance from the highest mountain to the deepest hole on Earth is
only 17 miles, the Earth can't match the roughness of an enlarged
golf ball.

The Earth *is* flattened at the poles by about 25 miles. This seems
like a great deal, but compared to the 8,000-mile diameter of the
Earth, this flattening is about half the depth of one of the dimples on
the golf ball's surface.

Magma is often said to be "liquid," but it compares more closely
to Turkish taffy. If you twist Turkish taffy slowly, it will bend. If you
put it into a container and wait awhile, it will conform to the shape

Subject Matter Review (continued)

of the container just like a liquid. However, if you twist it quickly, taffy will break. If you hit it with a hammer, it will shatter like glass.

Finding a comparison to the continental plates is a little harder. Imagine a river 70 feet deep with a foot of ice on top. The bottom of the river represents the center of the Earth.

In the spring, when the ice breaks up and starts to flow, it does many of the things the continental plates do. Chunks of ice grind together and slide over and under each other. The ones that slide under another gradually melt into the warmer water below.

This example breaks down when you think of the speed at which the river flows and how quickly it changes. In order to get a scale of the time, spring would have to be several hundred thousand years long.

(You may want to go back now and read this passage in the normal way.)

Answers:

  1. 2   2. 2   3. 5   4. 1   5. 3

CHECK YOUR
ANSWERS

Chapter
Nine
Science

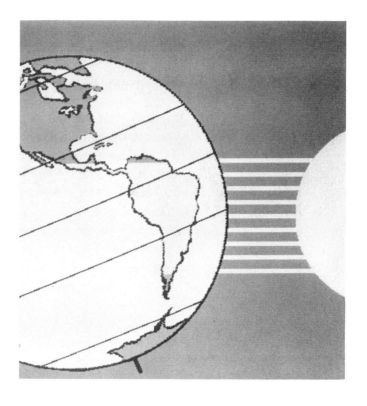

Preview of the Video

In this lesson, we'll be looking for main ideas and the supporting details. Because of the nature of the material, we also will emphasize the skill of comparing and contrasting.

This program begins with a fairly detailed description of the air around us. Just what is the atmosphere like? What keeps the chemistry of the air in balance so it can support life on our planet?

Pay particular attention to the illustrations of the layers of atmosphere. Why do these few miles of air make us unique? How many life-giving purposes does it serve?

You'll find this section of the video to be more than the evening weather report from the local TV channel.

When we move out into the solar system and beyond, we find a scale of space and time so enormous that it's a miracle the frail mind of the human has ever been able to piece the information together.

You may not agree with all the ideas in this program. That's great! Do keep an open mind, though, and recognize that the ideas of science change all the time. In fact, the video mentions some "truths" of science that had to give way to new "truths."

Goal-Setting Exercise for Program 9

Read these short selections and answer the questions.

If you ask 10 people what the boiling point of water is, eight will say it's 212°. One of them will say it's 100°, and one will say, "I don't know." All three answers are correct.

Water boils at 212° Fahrenheit or 100° Celsius *at sea level*. Those who say they don't know are right, too, because the temperature at which water boils depends on the atmospheric pressure. The less pressure, the lower the temperature required to evaporate water. Water will get no hotter than boiling.

In the vacuum of space—where there is no pressure—blood, which is mostly water, boils at body temperature.

1. Boiling an egg on top of Mount Everest would be
   1) easier because water would boil at less than 212° F.
   2) easier because there is less air pressure.
   3) more difficult because the water would boil before it was hot enough to cook the egg.
   4) more difficult because there is more air pressure the higher you go.
   5) none of the above

   1. ① ② ③ ④ ⑤

2. A pressure cooker
   1) cooks better than most other methods.
   2) heats water to more than 212° F because it increases the pressure.
   3) works on a principle no one really understands.
   4) causes a vacuum inside, which makes things cook at a lower temperature.
   5) decreases the pressure but increases the temperature.

   2. ① ② ③ ④ ⑤

Goal-Setting Exercise for Program 9 (continued)

3. Sulfur is mined by melting it with hot water. Sulfur melts at 440° F. This temperature can be reached only by

    1) increasing the pressure.

    2) decreasing the pressure.

    3) supplying a great deal of heat energy.

    4) 1) and 2) but not 3)

    5) 1) and 3) but not 2)

3. ① ② ③ ④ ⑤

4. Distilled water is produced by boiling water and condensing the vapor back into liquid form. A vacuum still is often used because

    1) it's better.

    2) it makes purer water.

    3) the water boils at a lower temperature so it takes less fuel.

    4) 1), 2), and 3)

    5) 1) and 2) but not 3)

4. ① ② ③ ④ ⑤

Many stargazers wonder why they see fewer meteors before midnight than after.

No, the meteors aren't on a time schedule. The effect has to do with the rotation of the Earth. In the evening hours, we see only those very fast meteors that catch up to us from the rear. After midnight, our speed changes in relation to the meteor field because our rotation is facing the same direction as our orbit. From the point of view of the meteors, we are going much faster than we were before midnight. We get not only the ones that overtake us but *also* the ones we overtake.

Think about this the next time you drive in a rainstorm. More drops hit the windshield than the rear window.

5. According to this article, we are "going faster" in the morning because

    1) our rotation speed is added to our orbital speed.

    2) the Earth turns faster in the early morning.

    3) more meteors overtake us in the morning.

    4) meteors travel faster in the morning.

    5) There isn't sufficient information to know for sure.

5. ① ② ③ ④ ⑤

Goal-
Setting
Exercise
for
Program 9
(continued)

6. Wedding guests are throwing rice at the bride   6. ① ② ③ ④ ⑤
   and groom, who are standing on a moving
   carousel. Which of the following can you
   conclude?
   1) More rice will hit them because they are
      moving.
   2) Less rice will hit them.
   3) The same amount of rice will hit them as
      if they were standing still.
   4) More rice will hit them in the face than
      on the back of the head.
   5) There isn't enough information to make
      any of the above conclusions.

Answers for Goal-Setting Exercise:

1. 3	2. 2	3. 5
4. 3	5. 1	6. 5

CHECK YOUR
ANSWERS

**Viewing
Prescription
for
Program 9**

❑ If you got them **all right** …   you're getting better all the time.
                                         Listen for some new ideas in the
                                         video.

❑ If you missed one or more …   all of these questions require you to
                                         draw a conclusion or anticipate an
                                         outcome. If you missed more than two
                                         of these questions, review the section
                                         of this chapter on *inference patterns*.

Vocabulary for Program 9

atmosphere (AT-mohs-fear) is the name given to the complete air mass surrounding the Earth.

troposphere (TROAP-us-fear) is the first layer of air in the atmosphere. It is said to extend 7 to 10 miles high.

stratosphere (STRAT-ohs-fear) is the next higher level. The air is thin and no weather occurs. Jets fly at this level.

mesosphere (MEZ-ohs-fear) is the next higher level. Hardly any air exists at this level.

exosphere (EX-ohs-fear) is the last level of the atmosphere we count. Though the atmosphere doesn't completely stop, at this level it is virtually a vacuum.

axial (AX-ee-uhl) refers to an axis or pivot point.

ozone (OH-zone) is a form of oxygen that has three atoms linked together. There is a protective layer of this gas in the atmosphere.

mean (MEEN) is a numerical average.

doldrums (DOHL-drums) refers to a part of the oceans where there is a light wind. It can also mean a lazy or inactive time. If you say, "I'm in the doldrums," it probably means you're listless.

barometer (buh-RAHM-uh-tuhr) is an instrument for measuring the air pressure of the atmosphere.

mass (MASS), in science, refers to the amount of matter something contains. Scientists make a distinction between mass and weight. Weight depends on the effect gravity has on mass.

leeward refers to the sheltered side of something. As it is used in this chapter, it means sheltered from the wind.

light-Year is one of the measuring sticks for the universe. It is the distance light travels in a year.

LEARN THE WORDS

NOW WATCH PROGRAM 9

Subject Matter Review

1. The Earth's atmosphere is a mixture of gases. Two of them, nitrogen and oxygen, make up more than 90% of the atmosphere.
2. For purposes of discussion, the atmosphere has four levels: troposphere, stratosphere, mesosphere, and exosphere.
3. The ozone layer, part of the stratosphere, protects us from harmful ultraviolet light.
4. Air pressure decreases the farther from Earth you go.
5. The rotation of the Earth influences wind patterns.
6. Seasonal temperature differences are a result of the tilting of the Earth, which causes the sun's rays to strike the surface more directly in warm months.
7. Individually, the planets are unlike each other, yet they fall into two classifications. The terrestrial planets are much like the Earth. The "gas giants" (sometimes call Jovian) are somewhat like each other but not like the Earth.
8. Distances in the universe are so vast they have an abstract quality.
9. The universe is filled with billions upon billions of stars.

**LEARN THE
FACTS**

THE WORLD ACCORDING TO TOM

For the average guy, the scientific argument over the difference between mass and weight seems a little silly. It might be, too, if nothing ever left the Earth. Since someone may ask you about it sometime, even if you've gone this long and escaped the argument, let's set up an example so you'll understand the scientific difference for sure.

Let's imagine you weigh exactly the same as your friend Joe. If you and Joe sat on either side of a teeter-totter, you'd exactly balance (or "set the table," as we used to say as kids.) If you both stand on a set of bathroom scales, you'll both weigh the same. Let's say you weigh 180 pounds. (I just picked that number because it's easy to divide by six, which I will want to do shortly.)

Now, you and Joe get the rare opportunity to go to the moon. For some reason beyond my comprehension, you take along the teeter-totter and the bathroom scales.

After a few days of "weightlessness" while you're falling toward the moon, you arrive at your lunar destination. Being "teetermani-acs," you immediately set up your balance beam. You and Joe still balance. Then you stand on the bathroom scales, and you find you each weigh only 30 pounds. (The moon's gravity is one-sixth that of

**PRACTICE
THE SKILLS**

the Earth. Got it?) You're still as big as you were. Your mass hasn't changed. Mass never changes. Only the weight does because weight depends on the effect gravity has on your mass.

Signed: Tom

Now answer these questions:

1. Which of the following would best tell the **style** in which this passage is written?   1. ① ② ③ ④ ⑤
   1) formal
   2) colloquial
   3) informal
   4) satirical
   5) scientific

2. Which of the following is the best title for this selection?   2. ① ② ③ ④ ⑤
   1) Weight and Mass Compared
   2) Teeter-Totters on the Moon
   3) The Gravity of the Moon
   4) The Gravity of the Earth
   5) Mass Communications

3. Which of the following is a **paraphrase** of the difference between mass and weight?   3. ① ② ③ ④ ⑤
   1) Mass doesn't change anywhere in the universe.
   2) Weight changes under certain circumstances.
   3) Mass is constant, but weight changes according to gravity.
   4) Mass and weight are the same thing.
   5) Weight doesn't change; only mass does.

4. You climb to the top of a 40-foot diving tower. You're standing on the bathroom scales. Joe pushes you and the scales off the tower, and you're standing on the scales all the way down. How much do the scales say you weigh?   4. ① ② ③ ④ ⑤
   1) 180 pounds
   2) 360 pounds
   3) 0 pounds
   4) 90 pounds
   5) 40 pounds

Subject Matter Review (continued)

5. This article strongly implies that   5. ① ② ③ ④ ⑤
   1) mass and weight are identical.
   2) weight is a constant.
   3) differences in mass and weight can't be measured.
   4) mass and weight aren't related.
   5) mass is an unchanging constant.

Answers:

1. 3   2. 1   3. 3

4. 3—The scale is falling at the same speed you are, so you have no weight. This is what "weightlessness" is. It's important to note that no one ever says "massless-ness"—mainly because there's no such thing.

5. 5—It is strongly implied, if not directly stated, that mass is unchanging.

CHECK YOUR ANSWERS

Now read this one.

> **Dear Editor,**
>
> Your recent article by "Tom" about mass and weight is an example of popular writing about science which creates many wrong ideas.
>
> To say that "mass never changes" is to admit appalling ignorance of the nature of matter. Mass is constantly being changed, destroyed, and created, producing differences in masses and energy. The sun alone "changes" 7 billion kilograms of mass into energy *every second* of Earth time. Think of the millions upon millions of stars in the universe changing untold amounts of mass into energy. Mass conversion is a commonplace event.
>
> Writers like Tom who present such simplistic views would contribute more to the field of science if they wrote about politics.
>
> **Signed: Ex-Reader**

PRACTICE THE SKILLS

Now answer these questions:

1. Comparing this passage with the last one, the   1. ① ② ③ ④ ⑤
   latter could be said to be more
   1) informal
   2) colloquial
   3) formal
   4) neutral
   5) simplistic

Subject Matter Review (continued)

2. Which of the following is a fact according to "Ex-Reader"?   2. ① ② ③ ④ ⑤
   1) Mass is the same as weight.
   2) Mass can be and is changed.
   3) Tom should do something else for a living.
   4) Tom's article is imprecise.
   5) Popular writers give the wrong impression about science.

3. Looking at the situation as "Ex-Reader" does, you could say   3. ① ② ③ ④ ⑤
   1) Tom has no business reporting about things scientific.
   2) one questionable statement makes Tom's article worthless.
   3) science is too important to be dealt with in "simplistic" terms.
   4) everyone knows that nuclear reactions change mass.
   5) all of the above

Answers:
1. 3   2. 2   3. 2

CHECK YOUR ANSWERS

PRACTICE THE SKILLS

Now read Tom's next column.

THE WORLD ACCORDING TO TOM

Golly, Mr. Ex-Reader, I apologize for insulting your remarkable intelligence. Your criticism leaves me a little gun-shy, though, because in this column I'm going to talk about measure, and I'll surely call a light-year a "simplistic" yardstick.

If you want to guess the exact day our race started measuring things, you're welcome to it. Whenever it was, on day two we made two measuring discoveries of greater importance. First, you need more than one unit. The second joint of the index finger may be OK to tell the length of a saber-toothed tiger's tooth, but not to tell how far it is to your neighbor's cave. (Steps would be better.) Another part of this discovery is that it's nice if the units are related in some way. (So many knuckles make a hand, so many hands make a step.)

Second, we realized the need for some kind of standardization. A unit always has to be the same. (Rubber bands don't make good measuring tapes.) Once measuring had begun, it became addictive. We had to measure *everything*. For big things, we invented big units. For small things, we came up with the tiniest units imaginable.

When we looked to the heavens, the distances were so great we needed a very large yardstick. Enter the light-year. The speed of light is always the same (therefore, standard). If I knew how far it travels in a year, I could use it as a measure that would always be the same. I do know! Light travels 186,200 miles a second or 5,880,000,000,000 miles in a year. Now I have a yardstick of great length that should allow me to measure anything, right? I can say one light-year and get rid of all those zeros.

Unhappily, a light-year is still too short for space. It's easy to find something in the universe that's 5,000,000 light-years from Earth, and we're right back into the zero business.

In looking for yet a larger unit, the "parsec" was invented. This unit is derived from trigonometry. It's based on the way a star appears to change location when viewed from two different places in the Earth's orbit.

Try this to help you understand a parsec. Place your thumb about five inches in front of your nose. Sight the wall over your thumb. Close first one eye, then the other. Your thumb will appear to move on the background of the wall. (Sorry for the simplistic explanation, Ex-Reader.) The angle at which you look at your thumb is called a parallax. Now move your thumb farther away from your nose and repeat the process. Notice that your thumb doesn't seem to move as far as it did. At arm's length, your thumb hardly moves at all. If your arm were long enough, you couldn't measure the angle between your eye and your thumb in degrees. It would be too small. You'd have to use minutes or even seconds, parallax seconds or parsecs.

Imagine that your left eye is the Earth on the first day of spring. Your nose is the sun, 93.5 million miles away, and beyond that another 93.5 million miles is your right eye, representing the position of the Earth on the first day of fall. Your thumb is a star millions of miles away. Viewed from these two extremes in the Earth's orbit, the star's position will seem to shift ever so slightly. By measuring these tiny shifts in apparent location, scientists can calculate the distance in parsecs.

Without going into the whole thing, a parsec is 3.26 light-years, but still too small to measure intergalactic space.

We'll take up the solution to this problem next time.

Signed: Tom

Subject Matter Review
(continued)

1. This selection is mainly about   1. ① ② ③ ④ ⑤
   1) parsecs
   2) light-years
   3) measure
   4) distance in space
   5) mathematics in science

2. The tone of this passage is   2. ① ② ③ ④ ⑤
   1) serious
   2) informal
   3) silly
   4) formal
   5) scientific

3. Make a list of the different kinds of measure
   either directly mentioned or implied in this
   selection.

   _____
   _____
   _____
   _____
   _____

4. If you were in charge of developing a measure
   larger than a parsec, what would you do?

   _____
   _____
   _____
   _____
   _____

5. You are asked to make an inference about the
   division of the units used in measuring
   angles. What are those units? Do you know how
   many of each unit makes the next larger?

   _____
   _____
   _____
   _____
   _____

Subject Matter Review (continued)

Answers:
1. 3   2. 2

CHECK YOUR ANSWERS

Just for Fun

You can amaze your friends with your new information about parsecs. The same principle can be used to estimate distance on Earth.

The length of your arm is 10 times the distance between your eyes. Hold your thumb at arm's length and sight over it just as described earlier. Estimate the distance your thumb seems to move on the background of whatever you are looking at. Multiply this distance by 10, and that's how far away you are from the object you are sighting. Here's an example:

With your arm extended to its full length, sight at a picture on the wall. You know the picture is one foot across. As you sight it, closing first one eye and then the other, your thumb moves exactly from one side of the picture to the other. Your thumb has seemed to move one foot, so you are 10 feet from the picture. With a little practice, you can easily measure distances up to a mile or so.

Test-Taking Tip

You have noticed that many of the practice questions have as a possible answer "Not enough information to be certain" or something similar. You must take extreme care with such questions. Writers of tests use this response very often when there *is* sufficient information so you won't get the idea that every time you see this response it's the right answer. Example:

> **Five planets in our solar system, not including the Earth, were known in ancient times. The remaining three were discovered after the invention of the telescope. The final one to be discovered was known to exist long before it was actually seen.**
>
> **How many planets are there?**
>   1) 5
> * 2) 9
>   3) 13
>   4) 8
>   5) There isn't enough information to be sure.

The answer is 2. There are nine planets: five known in ancient times, plus Earth, plus three discovered after the invention of the telescope.

Subject Matter Review (continued)

The last planet to be discovered was

    1) Neptune

    2) Saturn

    3) Pluto

    4) Jupiter

  * **5) There isn't enough information to be sure.**

The correct answer to the second question is 5—because nowhere in the passage does it say anything about the names of the planets. *Even if you know that the last planet to be discovered was Pluto, answer 5 is still the best answer to this question.*

Read this selection and answer the questions.

PRACTICE THE SKILLS

    It's widely known that atmospheric pressure, which is about 15 pounds per square inch at sea level, is the result of the weight of the air above us. Since we are at the bottom of a huge mass of air, our bodies are subjected to about 20 tons of weight. The only thing that keeps us from being crushed is the amount of air inside us to balance out this pressure.

    Less understood is the air pressure inside an enclosed vessel. Imagine a pressure tank of reasonable size. Do you think you could pump enough air into the tank to increase its weight 15 pounds? It's doubtful. What does it mean to have 90 pounds of air pressure in a tank if it isn't a measurement of the weight of the air?

    Imagine the air in the tank as individual molecules. They are whizzing around inside the tank, colliding with the sides. Each time a molecule hits the tank and bounces off, it exerts pressure on the side of the tank. The more molecules in the tank, the more opportunity for collision. What you are really measuring when you check the pressure in your tires is the force it takes to turn the molecules around.

Now answer the questions.

1. According to the passage, the weight of air in the atmosphere

    1) is always the same.

    2) exerts a huge force on our bodies.

    3) is equal to the pressure inside our bodies.

    4) 1) and 2) but not 3)

    5) 2) and 3) but not 1)

1. ① ② ③ ④ ⑤

2. Your ears sometimes "pop" when you're driving   2. ① ② ③ ④ ⑤
    in the mountains. This is because
    1) mountains are high.
    2) there's something wrong with your ears.
    3) the pressure is different inside your
        body than outside.
    4) air pressure is greater the higher you
        go.
    5) There isn't enough information to be
        certain.

3. Comparing the third paragraph to the rest of   3. ① ② ③ ④ ⑤
    the article, it could be said
    1) a lot of air can be pumped into a tank.
    2) air in a tank has pressure for a
        different reason than air in the open
        atmosphere.
    3) the third paragraph paraphrases the first
        two.
    4) No comparison can be made.
    5) All of the paragraphs are about the same
        thing.

4. Suppose you dropped marbles at a constant   4. ① ② ③ ④ ⑤
    rate on a set of scales. Each time a marble
    hits the scales and bounces off, the scales
    will register weight. You increase the height
    at which you drop the marbles and you observe
    1) greater weight the farther the marbles
        fall.
    2) less weight the farther the marbles fall.
    3) the same weight regardless of distance.
    4) none of the above
    5) There isn't enough information to be
        certain.

5. A tank of compressed air is heated, adding
   energy to the molecules so they move faster.
   In this case,
   1) there would be more and harder collisions
      and greater pressure.
   2) there would be fewer collisions and less
      pressure.
   3) the tank would weigh more.
   4) hot air is lighter, so the tank would
      weigh less.
   5) none of the above

5. ① ② ③ ④ ⑤

Thought question:

Why do you suppose there is a warning on pressurized spray cans telling you not to throw them into
a fire?

Answers:

  1. 5   2. 3   3. 2   4. 1   5. 1

Thought Question: If a pressurized can is heated, the gas pressure increases accordingly.
The increased pressure can cause the can to explode when the can can't hold the pressure
anymore. This is why many "spray" cans have labels warning us to keep them away from
heat.

CHECK YOUR
ANSWERS

Chapter
Ten
Science

This program gives you a glimpse at the most basic unit of matter—the atom.

The power of the atom was suspected for centuries, but is was 1945 before we succeeded in harnessing it.

As you watch the program, keep in mind that no one has ever seen an atom. What we understand about atomic science has come to us from centuries of study, thought, and experimentation.

Nuclear physics, or the study of the atom, is based on mathematical theories.

The second part of the program is about chemistry. Combinations of atoms, in some form or another, produce *everything*: from your shoestrings to the toast you had for breakfast, from the roses in your garden to a jet plane.

Goal-Setting Exercise for Program 10

The ball is on the five-yard line. The defending team commits an infraction of the rules that should cost it a 15-yard penalty. However, because of the position of the ball, the team is penalized only half the distance to the goal line. If the defenders are penalized again, the ball is moved half the *remaining* distance to the goal and so on.

1. The game referred to in this paragraph is   1. ① ② ③ ④ ⑤
   1) soccer
   2) volleyball
   3) football
   4) lacrosse
   5) cricket

2. Under these conditions, how many consecutive   2. ① ② ③ ④ ⑤
   penalties would result in a score?
   1) 2
   2) 3
   3) 4
   4) 12
   5) They never would.

3. The "five-yard" rule exists in this game   3. ① ② ③ ④ ⑤
   1) so the offensive team can score.
   2) so the offensive team cannot score by
      penalties alone.
   3) because the defensive team needs a better
      chance.
   4) because it's the only way the referees
      can keep track of the ball.
   5) because it's the way the game is played.

Goal-Setting Exercise for Program 10 (continued)

Radioactive elements give up their radioactivity at a constant rate. After a given period of time, they lose half their radioactivity. Each element has its own rate of decay. Carbon 14, for example, loses half its radioactivity in 5,700 years. Iron 53 loses half its radioactivity fairly rapidly, in about 9 minutes.

4. A radioactive element loses all its radioactivity in

    4. ① ② ③ ④ ⑤

   1) 5,700 years
   2) 9 minutes
   3) between 9 minutes and 5,700 years
   4) both 1) and 2)
   5) It never does.

5. You could conclude that the radioactive waste from nuclear reactors

    5. ① ② ③ ④ ⑤

   1) eventually would lose all its radioactivity.
   2) does not follow the same pattern as natural radioactivity.
   3) will always contain some radioactivity.
   4) will lose its radioactivity at an ever-increasing rate.
   5) will never be safe.

Answers for Goal-Setting Exercise:
  1. 3   2. 5   3. 2   4. 5   5. 3

CHECK YOUR ANSWERS

Viewing Prescription for Program 10

❑ If you got them **all right** …
    you are either a great scientist or a great sports fan.

❑ If you missed number **1** …
    are you still having trouble finding *inferred main ideas*? Pay close attention to the reading selections in the video.

❑ If you missed number **2** …
    many *details* in this video must be inferred. Watch for them. The workbook examples should help.

❑ If you missed number **4** …
    this paragraph parallels the first. Be sure you complete the exercises on *analogies* on the Extra Practice page for this chapter.

❑ If you missed number **5** …
    the video will help you understand this concept.

Vocabulary for Program 10

atom (AT-uhm) is the smallest piece of something that still has the characteristics of the thing you started with.

matter (MAT-tuhr) is anything that has weight and takes up space. While the weight may change, if it's made of atoms—it's matter.

element (ELL-uh-ment), as used in this lesson, refers to the chemical elements. They are all the *pure* substances we know about: gold, oxygen, hydrogen, carbon, and all the others.

electron (ee-LECK-trahn) is a particle in an atom with a negative electrical charge.

proton (PRO-tahn) is a positively charged particle in an atom.

neutron (NEW-trahn) is a particle in an atom with no electrical charge.

nucleus (NEW-klee-us) is thought of as the center of the atom. It contains the particles involved in nuclear power. The plural of nucleus is *nuclei* (NEW-klee-eye).

LEARN THE WORDS

Vocabulary for Program 10 (continued)

fission (FIZH-uhn) means to split. In this lesson, it refers to the process of breaking apart the nucleus of an atom.

fusion (FEWZH-uhn) means to put together. It refers to the combining of atoms. Energy is released when nuclear fusion takes place.

uranium (you-RAIN-ee-uhm) is a heavy element used in producing nuclear energy.

isotope (EYE-soh-toap) refers to the different forms of an element. Isotopes of an element have the same atomic number but different atomic weights.

deuterium (dew-TEAR-ee-uhm) is an isotope of hydrogen. It is also called "heavy hydrogen." It's used in nuclear fusion.

NOW
WATCH
PROGRAM
10

**Subject
Matter
Review**

Subject Matter Review

1. The atoms of an element are chemically identical.
2. Atoms contain three types of particles: electrons, protons, and neutrons.
3. An atom is mostly empty space.
4. There are two kinds of nuclear reactions: fission and fusion
5. Deuterium, the fuel for nuclear fusion, exists in great quantities in sea water.
6. Radioactive decay is used as a clock to determine the age of ancient civilizations and earth structures.
7. Chemistry investigates the way elements go together to form the different substances we know about.
8. Compounds result from chemical action in which electrons are either traded or shared.
9. Atoms cannot be changed chemically.

LEARN THE
FACTS

Paraphrasing

A good way to remember science material is to paraphrase it in the form of a simple story. We have done this several times in this book. The football "five-yard" rule compared to the radioactive half-life is one example. As you read, look for examples you can rewrite in the same way.

In the space below, retell the chain reaction story from the video as if you were setting dominoes on end and knocking them down. You'll need to describe how to set them up to get an uncontrolled reaction. How would you set them up differently to demonstrate a controlled reaction?

_____
_____
_____
_____
_____
_____
_____
_____
_____
_____
_____
_____
_____
_____
_____
_____

PRACTICE
THE SKILLS

Subject Matter Review (continued)

Reading Charts

Scientists spend most of their time looking things up. Below is a chart of scientific information. Study it and answer the questions.

PRACTICE THE SKILLS

NAME	DATES	CONTRIBUTION
Democritus Greece	460 B.C.	The idea of atoms.
John Dalton England	1766–1844	System of chemical notation.
J.J. Berzelius Sweden	1779–1848	Developed modern alphabetical chemical notation.
D. Mendeleev Russia	1834–1907	Classified the elements.
J.J. Thomson 1856–1940 England	1856-1940	Stated the nature of the atom.
N. Bohr Denmark	1885–1962	Developed the idea of the planetary atom model.
F.W. Aston England	1887–1945	Discovered and explained isotopes.
H. Moseley England	1801–1872	First used atomic number.
A.H. Becquerel France	1852–1908	Discovered and explained radioactivity.
E. Fermi America (Born: Italy)	1901–1954	Discovered neutron bombardment.
E.O. Lawrence America	1901–1958	Designed the cyclotron; the "atom smasher."
A. Einstein America (Born: Germany)	1879–1955	Discovered the mathematics of nuclear energy: $E=mc^2$
J.R. Oppenheimer America	1904–1967	Clarified concept of anti-particle; supervised the building of the "atom bomb."

Now anwer these questions.

1. ① ② ③ ④ ⑤

1. Which of the following could be concluded
   from this chart?
   1) Atomic theory is a very recent develop-
      ment.
   2) No one country can claim exclusive rights
      to atomic discoveries.
   3) All atomic discoveries were made in the
      20th century.
   4) Chemistry and physics are unrelated.
   5) Mathematics is related to physics but not
      to chemistry.

2. ① ② ③ ④ ⑤

2. Looking at the contributions listed, which of
   the following quotations by scientists *best*
   tells the main idea?
   1) Newton: "I have accomplished what I have
      only by standing on the shoulders of sci-
      entific giants before me."
   2) Einstein: "I don't know what the weapons
      of World War III will be, but the next
      one will be fought with rocks."
   3) Archimedes: "Give me a lever long enough
      and a prop strong enough. I can single-
      handed move the world."
   4) Edison: "Genius is one percent inspira-
      tion and ninety-nine percent perspira-
      tion."
   5) Bohr: "Every sentence I utter must be
      understood not as an affirmation, but a
      question."

3. ① ② ③ ④ ⑤

3. J.R. Oppenheimer supervised the building of
   the first atomic bomb, but the chart says he
   1) didn't recognize the power of the atom.
   2) was questioned about his patriotism.
   3) doubted that humans were capable of han-
      dling this great new power.
   4) died before an atomic bomb was exploded.
   5) none of the above

**CHECK YOUR
ANSWERS**

**Subject
Matter
Review**
(continued)

Answers:
1. 2
2. 1—All the others are good expressions of scientific thought, but they don't apply.
3. 5

The Scientific Method

Science is, among other things, a way of thinking. Scientists try to use known information in logical ways to learn about the unknown. Over the centuries, this way of thinking has come to be known as "The Scientific Method." Below is an exercise in scientific thinking.

> **Bill is one of the more absent-minded people around. He went to the store this morning and bought something which the clerk sealed in a paper bag.**
> **Poor Bill! He forgot what was in the bag, but he is too embarrassed to admit it. Rather than simply looking in the bag, utterly destroying his pride, he has decided to apply the scientific method to determine the contents.**

PRACTICE

Give Bill some help by suggesting answers to the following questions.

1. What's the problem? _____
   _____

2. How can he collect information about the
   problem? _____
   _____

3. How can he narrow down the possibilities? ____
   _____

4. How can he test the possibilities? _____
   _____

5. What will he learn from his test? _____
   _____

6. What must Bill do after he's observed,
   tested, and thought? _____
   _____

Answers:
This is an exercise in the steps to the "Scientific Process." The "steps" are underlined. Your solutions to Bill's dilemma may be different from ours, but make sure your steps are the same.

1. <u>State the problem</u>: What's in the bag?
2. <u>Collect information</u>: Bill could do lots of things. He could try to remember why he went to the store in the first place. Did the clerk give him a receipt? He could even swallow his pride and go back and ask the clerk.
3. <u>Form a hypothesis</u>: What does Bill *think* is in the bag?
4. <u>Observe and experiment</u>: He can pinch, shake, smell, weigh, or squeeze the bag.
5. <u>Interpret the results</u>: Bill will want to think about what the results of his test tell him about the contents of the bag.
6. <u>Draw conclusions</u>: Eventually, Bill must decide—once and for all—what he believes is in the bag … or he may conclude that he does not know.

Although not formally included in the scientific method, two more steps are common to scientific investigations:

A. <u>Communicate the results</u>: With this much information, Bill, being a true scientist, should feel obligated to share the secrets he has uncovered with all the other absent-minded individuals in the world.
B. <u>List new problems</u>: What about other bags and other times? What about boxes instead of bags? What about atoms?

It is important to remember the difference between Bill's situation and the situation usually facing real scientists: Bill *could* just open the bag and look inside; most scientists can't do that. The conclusions they draw from the scientific method are the only way scientists have of deciding "what's in the bag."

CHECK YOUR ANSWERS

Using the information above and your own logic, fill out the chart below with the steps to the scientific process *in proper sequence*. (Just the letter assigned to each step will do.)

A. Observe and experiment.
B. State the problem.
D. Collect information.
C. Interpret the results.
E. Form hypothesis.

F. List new problems.
G. Communicate results and check the hypothesis.
H. Draw conclusions.

PRACTICE

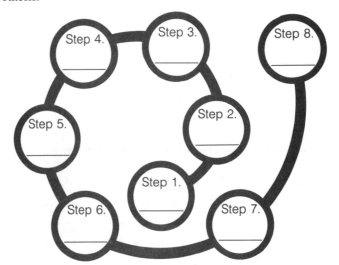

Now answer these questions.

1. ① ② ③ ④ ⑤

1. According to this chart,
   1) only one hypothesis is checked out at a time.
   2) all questions can be answered this way.
   3) there is no specific sequence.
   4) only scientists are allowed to use this system.
   5) all of the above

2. ① ② ③ ④ ⑤

2. A good hypothesis should
   1) answer all the questions about the problem.
   2) inspire new questions.
   3) lead to a conclusion that is always true.
   4) 2) and 3) but not 1)
   5) 1) and 3) but not 2)

3. ① ② ③ ④ ⑤

3. Why is it important to communicate the results of a scientific study?
   1) People are interested in such things.
   2) so other people can check them out.
   3) Researchers benefit from the information that others have discovered.
   4) 1) and 2) but not 3)
   5) 2) and 3) but not 1)

Answers:
1. 1   2. 2   3. 5

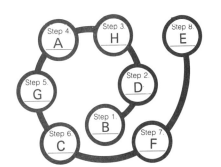

CHECK YOUR
ANSWERS

1. ① ② ③ ④ ⑤

Subject
Matter
Review
(continued)

Here's a chance for you to do some "research" on your own. Below is a list of things that *aren't* what they're called. You may need to collect information from several sources to find out what they really are. Try finding out about the questions by looking in dictionaries or encyclopedias.

PRACTICE

1. tin can _____

_____

2. pencil lead _____

_____

3. power company _____

_____

4. nickel (five-cent piece) _____

_____

5. silver dollar _____

_____

Answers:
1. Tin cans are made of steel. They merely have a thin tin coating to keep them from rusting.
2. Pencil lead isn't made of lead, but of graphite (a form of carbon).
3. Power companies don't sell power. To a scientist, power is work done over a period of time. Utility companies sell you the energy so *you* can produce the power.
4. "Nickels" have always been made of 75 parts copper and only 25 parts nickel— except during WWII, when nickels contained no nickel at all.
5. Silver dollars have never been pure silver. The silver is alloyed (mixed) with copper to make the dollars wear better.

CHECK YOUR ANSWERS

Just for Fun

Try this as a conversation starter at a dull party. Bet someone that you can prove scientifically that it's impossible to walk across the room. It won't be hard to get some "takers."

Here's your proof. Before you can walk completely across the room, you have to walk half the distance. Before you can walk the rest of the way, you have to walk half of the remaining distance. Each half of a half gets increasingly smaller. Theoretically, what you say is true. The halves become infinitely tiny, but they are still there. Thought of in this way, it *is* impossible to walk across a room.

You may be able to swing the conversation over to the half-life of radioactive materials, nuclear power, hazardous waste, or some other topical subject. Even so, don't expect the tactic to improve your social life.

Subject Matter Review (continued)

Test-Taking Tip

Related to the test item that doesn't have enough information to answer the question is one that has too much. Passages that have irrelevant or extraneous information require a different kind of thinking. Example:

> **Scientists first thought oxygen weighed 8 times as much as hydrogen because 1 gram of hydrogen and 8 grams of oxygen always combined to form water. Later, it was discovered that oxygen is 16 times as heavy as hydrogen, so the atomic weight for hydrogen was arbitrarily set at 1 and oxygen at 16. By the same thinking, lithium was assigned a weight of 7, sulfur a weight of 32 and so on. A modern periodic table, however, lists hydrogen at 1.00797 and oxygen at 15.9994. The discrepancy is a result of existing isotopes.**

> **What is the lightest of all elements?**
> 1) **sulfur**
> * 2) **hydrogen**
> 3) **oxygen**
> 4) **lithium**
> 5) **none of the above**

The right answer is 2, but the reading passage is filled with information you don't need to come up with that answer.

Read these selections and answer the questions.

EXTRA PRACTICE

> **The general chemical rule is that an acid plus a base yields a salt. Hydrochloric acid, a compound of chlorine and hydrogen, combined with sodium hydroxide, a compound of the metal sodium and oxygen and hydrogen, mixed together produce sodium chloride and water.***
>
> $$HCl + NaOH = NaCl + H_2O$$
> **-OR-**
> **Hydrochloric Acid + Sodium Hydroxide = Sodium Chloride + Water**
>
> **Notice the replacement of the hydrogen and the hydroxide radical (OH), which produces water (H_2O), and the sodium and chlorine combining to produce sodium chloride. The replacement, in this case, takes place atom for atom to make the salt. *This* salt is table salt.**
>
> *** Remember that when elements are combined into compounds they lose their characteristics as elements.**

1. How much sodium hydroxide would it take to produce a pound of table salt?
   1) 1 pound
   2) 2 pounds
   3) $\frac{1}{2}$ pound
   4) 3 pounds
   5) There isn't enough information to tell.

1. ① ② ③ ④ ⑤

2. It can be inferred from this passage that
   1) table salt is manufactured by combining an acid and a base.
   2) chemical reactions always trade one atom for another.
   3) other acids and other bases produce salts.
   4) there is hydrochloric acid in table salt.
   5) there is metallic sodium in table salt.

2. ① ② ③ ④ ⑤

Heat transfers in three ways: conduction, convection, and radiation.

Conduction takes place by transferring the energy from molecule to molecule within the conductor. The handle of a skillet gets hot because the heat is "conducted" through the metal.

Convection relies on another medium to transfer the heat by currents. Everyone has seen Christmas angels on a pinwheel above a candle. The angels spin as a result of the current caused in the air by the candle.

Heat transfer by radiation means in the form of rays. In this form, heat is much like light. Woodburning stoves heat largely by radiation.

3. A vacuum bottle has a double wall of glass with air removed between the layers of glass. This helps keep your coffee warm because
   1) heat can't cause convection in the vacuum between the walls.
   2) conduction is minimized because the heat has no molecules of air to pass through.
   3) heat can't radiate through a vacuum.
   4) 1) and 3) but not 2)
   5) none of the above

3. ① ② ③ ④ ⑤

Subject
Matter
Review
(continued)

4. Vacuum bottles are coated with shiny silver   4. ① ② ③ ④ ⑤
because the mirror-like surface
1) prevents heat loss by conduction.
2) reflects the radiated heat back into the
interior of the bottle.
3) increases heat transfer by convection.
4) increases radiation.
5) decreases conduction but increases convection.

Answers:
   1. 5   2. 3   3. 2   4. 2

CHECK YOUR
ANSWERS

Chapter Eleven
Science

Activities in this chapter will be very different from what we've done in the past. We think you need a scheme for listening to information and making the same kind of mental judgments you've been making from written material.

Second, you'll do better on some tests if you know how they work. So we are providing the *actual answer sheet used at most GED testing centers* as an example. You can answer questions from this chapter by using the answer sheet.

Our third objective is to give you a chance to practice the test-taking suggestions mentioned in the last chapter. Since there isn't anyone to time you, you may want to set a limit for yourself. The video is 30 minutes long. You can probably do the work on the answer sheet in 10 minutes and answer the questions in about 40 minutes.

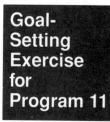

Goal-Setting Exercise for Program 11

Below is a successful Listening Formula. Study it carefully and then watch the video.

Listening Formula

1. **Listen with a purpose.**

   It may come as no surprise to you that reasons for listening sound like the list of reading skills we've spent so much time on. At the simplest level, you listen for literal meaning. At the most complex end of the list is listening for appreciation. For instructional purposes, start by asking yourself, "What do I want to get out of this?"

2. **Be mentally and physically prepared.**

   Comfort is necessary. Clearing your mind of outside influences is just as important. Experts say that listening requires a "listening space." This statement can be taken literally and figuratively.

3. **Concentrate on the main points.**

   Curiosity helps, but your mind can comprehend much more rapidly than a speaker can tell you things, so you might find you have a natural tendency to allow your mind to wander. DON'T LET IT! Focus your attention on the main points and, instead of "wandering," try to connect what is being said to something you already know.

   Good listening is like playing cat's cradle. You have to weave together what is being said and also connect it with knowledge you already have. One help is to anticipate what the speaker will say next. If you're right, you've made a connection. If you're wrong, you can modify what you were thinking. Keep directing your attention to the speaker's meaning.

4. **Watch the speaker.**

   In television, someone else has determined what you see. But facial expressions, gestures with the hands, and other "body language" will help you get a feel for the message.

5. **Decide whether to take notes.**

   Whether to take notes is totally up to the individual and may be determined by the purpose for listening. If you do take notes of instructional video, they should probably be very sketchy. If you concentrate too hard on your notes, you may lose the feel and forget why you were watching in the first place.

Apply these listening tips as you watch the video.

Subject Matter Review

Look at the answer sheet on page 177.

The actual GED answer sheet is not a part of the test booklet; it is a separate sheet onto which you must transfer your answers. This transferring process makes one more task for you to perform, and it must be accomplished accurately or your answers won't be graded correctly.

We'll go through each step of filling out the sample GED answer sheet in the workbook. This answer sheet is similar to those for many other standardized tests.

Remember: The answer sheet must be marked only with a soft lead pencil. Often pencils are furnished for tests such as this, but take your own along, just in case.

The steps for filling out the answer sheet are numbered so you can follow them.

PRACTICE THE SKILLS

Task 1

PRINT your name in the boxes provided at the top left-hand corner of the answer sheet: last name, space, first name, space, middle initial.

Below this set of boxes is a series of alphabets in little circles. Working from left to right, use a soft lead pencil to fill in the circles to *match* each letter of your name. The first row of circles is blank. Be certain you fill in one of the "blank" circles for every column where there is a blank in your name. (Note: Your name is printed so it can be read by people. If a machine scores your test, it will "read" the filled-in circles.)

Task 2

This task has two parts. Task 2a asks you to give the purpose, or reason, for taking the test. Task 2b asks you to tell whether you are on active duty with the military.

Task 3

For absolute identification, the test requires that you enter your Social Security number in the same way you entered your name. First write your number in the boxes, then fill in the corresponding numbered circles below. In each case, and throughout the test, be certain you fill in the circle *completely* with the pencil.

Task 4

Fill in the circles for your age.

Task 5

Fill in the highest grade you completed in school.

Subject
Matter
Review
(continued)

Task 6

Fill in the date (month, day, year) on which you are taking the test.

Task 7

If you were actually taking the GED test, you would enter the number from the front of your test booklet on this line. For this practice, fill in any number you want.

Task 8

The center giving the test may already have filled in the name of the testing center, or they may not need this information. Listen to the tester to see what is to be done.

Task 9

You must tell which of the GED test forms you are using so scores can be recorded properly. (If you were taking the GED test, you would find the form number on the test booklet or ask the tester.)

Task 10

For the GED exam, you would use a different answer sheet for each of the five parts of the test. Test 1 is Writing Skills, Test 2 is Social Studies, Test 3 is Science, Test 4 is Reading, and Test 5 is Math.

Task 11

When told to begin the test, look at the first question, choose an answer, and then fill in the circle on the answer sheet that matches the number of the answer you have selected for each question. The answer sheet is designed to record 80 answers, but most test sections have fewer questions than this.

Now answer these questions using your official answer sheet.

1. According to the video, copper was scarce during World War II because
   1) prices were high.
   2) it was being used as wire.
   3) it was being used for ammunition.
   4) mining operations were shut down.
   5) no one thought it was important.

2. Which of the following is *not* a reason to use copper in electricity?
   1) It is relatively cheap.
   2) It is a conductor.
   3) Wire can be made from it.
   4) Copper has good insulation quality.
   5) Wires made from copper last a long time.

3. Which of the following is the best insulator?
   1) rubber
   2) copper
   3) aluminum
   4) iron
   5) silver

4. Which of the following is the best general statement about magnetism?
   1) Magnetism has its origin in the atom.
   2) Gravity is the same as magnetism.
   3) The only way to get magnetism is through the use of electricity.
   4) Permanent magnets can be made of almost any material.
   5) Materials must be very cold to be magnetized.

5. Which of the following is *not* a state of matter?
   1) solid
   2) liquid
   3) gas
   4) plasma
   5) magnet

TESTS OF GENERAL EDUCATIONAL DEVELOPMENT (ged)

7 TEST BOOKLET NO.

8 TEST TAKEN AT

When completed this answer sheet must be treated as Confidential Material.

SCORE BOX

RAW SCORE	STD. SCORE	PERCENT. RANK	AVE. S.S.

9 TEST FORM

DO NOT MARK IN YOUR TEST BOOKLET

TEST ANSWERS

Fill in the circle corresponding to your answer for each question. Erase cleanly.

MN
MO
MP
MQ
MR
MS
MT
MU
MV
MW
MX
MY
MZ

SF
SG
SH
SJ
SK
SL
SM

10 TEST NUMBER

① ② ③ ④ ⑤

GED TESTING SERVICE OF THE AMERICAN COUNCIL ON EDUCATION

Trans-Optic® EB18-14511:3   A7300

1 BEGINNING AT THE LEFT BOX, PRINT YOUR LAST NAME, LEAVE A SPACE, FIRST NAME, SPACE, MIDDLE INITIAL.

2a PURPOSE FOR TESTING (Mark 1 or more)
EDUCATION ○   MILITARY ○
EMPLOYMENT ○   OTHER ○

2b ARE YOU ON ACTIVE DUTY IN THE ARMED FORCES?
YES ○   NO ○

3 SOCIAL SECURITY NUMBER

4 AGE

5 HIGHEST GRADE COMPLETED
6TH OR LOWER
7
8
9
10
11
12

6 TODAY'S DATE

	DAY	YEAR
JAN		1980
FEB	①	1981
MAR	②	1982
APR	③	1983
MAY		1984
JUNE		1985
JULY		1986
AUG		1987
SEPT		1988
OCT		1989
NOV		
DEC		

GEDTS FORM AS7010

6. The state of matter found most commonly in the universe is
   1) solid
   2) liquid
   3) gas
   4) plasma
   5) magnet

7. About the only place plasma is found on the Earth is in
   1) the oceans
   2) neon and fluorescent lights
   3) copper
   4) amber
   5) magnets

8. Which of the following did the video imply about gravity?
   1) It is the same throughout the universe.
   2) Newton was the first to recognize it.
   3) Gravity is the force which holds the universe together.
   4) Aristotle discovered the laws which govern gravity.
   5) Magnetism, electricity, and gravity are all the same thing.

9. A hockey puck sliding straight across the ice strikes the wall and bounces off at a predictable angle. Which is the *best* scientific explanation?
   1) Things which are at rest tend to remain at rest.
   2) Mass changes the force and acceleration of an object.
   3) The velocity of the puck is increased after striking the wall.
   4) Things in motion remain in motion in the same path unless an additional force is applied.
   5) Pucks travel rapidly on ice because there is little friction.

Subject Matter Review (continued)

10. Which of the following is *not* an example of the law of motion that says, "For every action there is an equal and opposite reaction"?

    1) When you step from a boat to the pier, the boat moves away and you step into the water.
    2) A rocket blasts a space shuttle into space.
    3) You fire a shotgun at a rabbit and the recoil leaves a bruise on your shoulder.
    4) A small girl swinging in a playground kicks the ground at the bottom of each swing.
    5) A spinning ping-pong ball curves across the net.

11. A football coach is talking to his linemen in the dressing room. They are about to meet a team with a much heavier line. Which of the following is the best scientific advice the coach could give his players?

    1) "Since you can't be heavier than they are, you've got to be going faster than they are."
    2) "Stand your ground."
    3) "Gain some weight."
    4) "Make sure you hit them straight on."
    5) "Remember, for every action there is an equal and opposite reaction."

Below are some excerpts from the video program. Read them and answer the
questions.

> Early humans were aware of electricity and its power. They could
> hardly have ignored it. The word electricity comes from the Greek
> word <u>electron</u>, which means amber—this rod is made of amber—
> fossilized tree sap.
> So what's the connection? The little scraps of paper stick to
> amber because of static electricity. Pretty much the same thing
> happens when your hair sticks to a comb or brush on a dry winter's
> day.

12. According to this passage, most of the words
    we associate with electricity come from
    1) static electricity
    2) a Greek word for amber
    3) a Greek word for comb
    4) paper
    5) none of the above

> In electric currents—like the one running your TV set—the
> electrons move in a constant stream. Electrons flow through these
> copper wires, but they won't move through the rubber insulation.
> Why is that? In some elements, the electrons move easily from atom
> to atom, making the electrical current flow quickly through the
> substance. That's what happens with this copper, so it's called a
> conductor. Most metals are conductors.

13. Which is the best conductor of electricity?
    1) plastic spoon
    2) ceramic bowl
    3) chrome-plated spatula
    4) wooden tongue depressor
    5) cotton glove

Subject Matter Review (continued)

All batteries produce direct current. But your house runs on alternating current (A.C.). This current changes direction 60 times every second. Electric companies use A.C. because it is cheaper to produce and transmit long-distance.

14. When discussing electrical current, it can be said that
    1) direct current always flows in the same direction.
    2) alternating current reverses its direction of flow.
    3) homes usually operate on A.C.
    4) A.C. is cheaper to produce and transmit than D.C.
    5) all of the above

We are now going to take a look at the most obvious and yet one of the most elusive parts of the physical world: matter.

Now, what exactly is matter? Most people would define matter sort of the way a Supreme Court justice described obscenity: "I can't define it, but I know it when I see it."

Matter is defined as anything that has weight and occupies space ... actually it's a word we use to describe the substances physical objects are made of.

15. "Elusive" means
    1) hard to understand
    2) sneaky
    3) easier to see than define
    4) obvious
    5) obscenity

Now read these selections, which were not in the video.

Many people use the term "dry cell" and "battery" interchangeably. To a scientist, there is a difference. "Cell" means one unit. A battery is made up of more than one cell. This is why the battery in your car is called a battery. It's made up of several cells connected together to produce the desired amount of energy. The six-volt *battery* in the lantern you take fishing with you contains four cells of 1-1/2 volts each.

16. You can infer that
    1) cells and batteries are the same thing.
    2) cells must be connected together to make electricity.
    3) batteries are used only in cars.
    4) "battery" means a series of similar devices connected together.
    5) None of these can be inferred.

Look at the way dry cells go into a flashlight. The case of the cell is the negative terminal. The little button on top is the positive. (See Fig. 1)

In a typical flashlight, the cells are arranged so the positive terminal touches, or makes contact with, a negative terminal. Cells arranged in negative-to-positive contact produce a *series circuit*. Cells connected in a series circuit give voltage equal to the sum of the voltage of each cell.

The flashlight pictured produces three volts.

Figure 2 is an arrangement of cells for a toy car. The car runs on 1-$1/2$ volts. The two cells are connected positive to positive and negative to negative. Parallel circuits of this type do not increase the voltage but increase the time the toy will run before the batteries must be changed.

FIG. 1

FLASHLIGHT (Series Circuit)

Spring (−)   (+)   (+)   Lamp

Bottom of Dry Cell (−)   Flashlight Case (−)

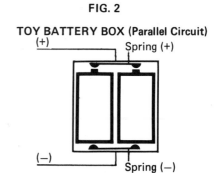

FIG. 2

TOY BATTERY BOX (Parallel Circuit)

(+)   Spring (+)

(−)   Spring (−)

17. The article doesn't state it, but can you
    figure out the voltage of one dry cell?
    1) 3
    2) $1\frac{1}{2}$
    3) $\frac{3}{4}$
    4) 1
    5) There isn't enough information to tell.

18. You have a flashlight like the one in Fig. 1,
    but it holds four dry cells. What is its
    voltage?
    1) 4
    2) 3
    3) $1\frac{1}{2}$
    4) 6
    5) 9

19. A portable radio operates on a series circuit
    of dry cells producing a total of 9 volts.
    How many dry cells does it take?
    1) 6
    2) 9
    3) 3
    4) 4
    5) 12

**Christmas tree lights are either series or parallel circuits. Re-
membering that current must flow from the plug and return, make
some judgments about the conditions illustrated below.**

FIG. 1
PARALLEL CHRISTMAS LIGHTS

PLUG   BURNED-OUT BULB

FIG. 2
SERIES CHRISTMAS TREE LIGHTS

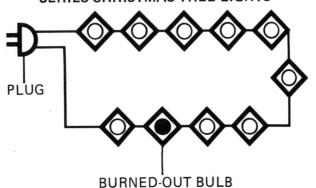

PLUG

BURNED-OUT BULB

Subject
Matter
Review
(continued)

20. Which of the following *best* describes this situation?
    1) Neither set of lights will work.
    2) None of the parallel lights will burn.
    3) None of the series lights will burn.
    4) All but one of the parallel lights will work but none of the series.
    5) All of the lights will burn except the burned-out ones.

21. You have a set of series lights with one bad bulb. You don't have a replacement bulb, so you remove the socket and wire the rest of the string together. Which of the following is the *best* answer to what will happen?
    1) The remaining bulbs will burn.
    2) The string still won't work.
    3) Some of the bulbs will burn; others won't.
    4) Because you have reduced the number of bulbs, they will last longer.
    5) The remaining bulbs will burn but will be much dimmer.

Simple machines work in predictable, mathematical ways. For instance, a lever three feet long resting on a spot one foot from the end yields a mechanical advantage of 2 to 1. That is, a weight of 100 pounds on the short end of the lever can be lifted by applying a force of 50 pounds on the long end of the lever. However, in order to raise the weight six inches, the long end of the lever must be depressed one foot.

Subject
Matter
Review
(continued)

22. Which of the following is supported by this passage?
    1) Machines can change the direction of a force.
    2) Machines can increase or multiply a force.
    3) If a machine increases the force, it must trade distance for that gain.
    4) What you get out of a machine is proportionate to what you put in.
    5) All of the above.

23. In Fig. 2, how far must the long end of the lever be depressed to raise the load one inch?
    1) 1 inch
    2) 4 inches
    3) 5 inches
    4) $\frac{1}{4}$ inch
    5) $\frac{1}{5}$ inch

Now check all the parts of your answer sheet with the one below.

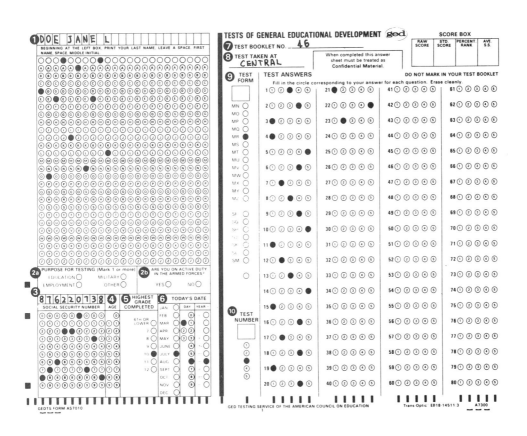

CHECK YOUR
ANSWERS

Test-Taking Tip

Before you do anything, be certain you have listened carefully to the instructions about using the answer sheet. At this point in the testing procedure, you can ask questions of the tester. *If you have any questions whatever about the procedures required in filling out the answer sheet—ask.*

Understanding the answer sheet will make you feel more comfortable while you take the test and may help you increase your score.

Chapter Twelve
Social Studies

The remaining lessons are designed to help you learn some of the "big ideas" in social studies and to help you learn to *read* better.

This program begins with the famous voyage of Columbus and goes through 300 years of our history, from "discovery" by Europeans to the end of the Revolutionary War. It covers the events, the people, and the politics that led to what we are today.

As you listen and watch, mentally practice those reading skills we have been learning. What is the main idea of a particular sequence? What details support this theme? Can you figure out unfamiliar words by listening to the other words around them?

Pay particular attention to the segment that discusses the ideas behind our form of government.

Goal-Setting Exercise for Program 12

Read these short passages and answer the questions.

Here is the famous quote from Thomas Paine as it appeared in his pamphlet "The Crisis."

These are the times that try men's souls. The summer soldier and the sunshine patriot will in this crisis shrink from the service of his country; but he that stands it NOW, deserves the love and thanks of man and woman. Tyranny, like hell, is not easily conquered; yet we have this consolation with us, that the harder the conflict, the more glorious the triumph. What we obtain too cheap, we esteem too lightly; 'tis dearness only that gives everything value. Heaven knows how to put a proper price upon its goods; and it would be strange indeed, if so celestial an article as FREEDOM should not be highly rated.

1. "The summer soldier and the sunshine patriot" refers to
   1) British soldiers
   2) Colonists who are willing to suffer and die for freedom
   3) less committed Colonists who will quit when the going gets tough
   4) Washington and Adams
   5) none of the above

1. ① ② ③ ④ ⑤

2. The quote "the harder the conflict, the more glorious the triumph" is most like which of the following expressions?
   1) No pain, no gain.
   2) The proof of the pudding is in the eating.
   3) Pride goes before a fall.
   4) Time cures all ills.
   5) A penny saved is a penny earned.

2. ① ② ③ ④ ⑤

Goal-
Setting
Exercise
for
Program 12
(continued)

3. Paine thinks freedom   3. ① ② ③ ④ ⑤
   1) will be easy to achieve.
   2) is very valuable.
   3) belongs to the summer soldier.
   4) is a form of tyranny.
   5) is hardly worth the effort.

**If Henry Wadsworth Longfellow had gotten his facts straight, his
most famous poem might have started like this:**

*Listen my children and give a pause
To the midnight ride of William Dawes*

It was William Dawes, a shoemaker, who started the famous ride
on that April night in 1775. He met Paul Revere, a silversmith, and
Samuel Prescott, a doctor, in Lexington, Massachusetts. By the time
the three of them got together, Dawes had already ridden several
miles alerting the Patriots to the threat of the British army.

The three riders started off toward Concord, but Revere and
Prescott were captured a short time later. Dawes was able to escape
and completed the daring ride.

Has Longfellow's choice of heroes affected our thinking? Revere's name is still connected with many fine products honoring the
memory of this 18th century craftsman. Did you ever hear of a pair
of shoes to commemorate the name of Dawes, the real hero of the
midnight ride?

4. This story of the famous midnight ride is   4. ① ② ③ ④ ⑤
   1) different from the traditional story.
   2) a more accurate account of what really
      happened.
   3) an attempt to discredit Paul Revere.
   4) an attempt to discredit Samuel Prescott.
   5) different, but possibly no more accurate
      than Longfellow's version.

5. In order for the above passage to make sense,   5. ① ② ③ ④ ⑤
   you have to know
   1) a great deal about Colonial history.
   2) about Paul Revere, William Dawes, and Sam
      Prescott.
   3) about the poem "Paul Revere's Ride" by
      H.W. Longfellow.
   4) that the Revolutionary War started in
      1775.
   5) the occupations of the three riders.

Goal-Setting Exercise for Program 12 (continued)

6. The author of this passage implies   6. ① ② ③ ④ ⑤
   1) Longfellow picked the wrong hero.
   2) our view of history is still affected by
      the Longfellow poem.
   3) it doesn't make any difference that the
      facts of the poem are inaccurate.
   4) 2) and 3) but not 1)
   5) 1) and 2) but not 3)

Answers for Goal-Setting Exercise:

1. 3	2. 1	3. 2
4. 5	5. 3	6. 5

CHECK YOUR ANSWERS

Viewing Prescription for Program 12

❑ If you got them **all right** …   three cheers for you! Enjoy the program and see if you can learn some new information about U.S. history.

❑ If you missed number **1** …   this program uses several ***figures of speech***. Be alert to them.

❑ If you missed number **2** …   you may need to practice ***inferring*** answers when there is more than one level of understanding. The work in this lesson should help you.

❑ If you missed number **3** …   understanding social studies material requires ***attention to details***. Review the listening suggestions in chapter eleven.

❑ If you missed number **4** …   be careful what you accept as ***fact***. The video deals with many facts and many bits of folklore. Be sure you can tell the difference.

Viewing Prescription for Program 12 (continued)

❑ If you missed number **5** … this question is based on *knowledge you already have*. Review what is said about interpreting cartoons in chapter five.

❑ If you missed number **6** … pay close attention to the way the video tells the story of the Salem witch trials.

Vocabulary for Program 12

Puritanism (PURE-uh-tun-izm) was the religion of the settlers of the Massachusetts Bay Colony. It was a very strict theology.

mercantilism (MURK-un-teel-izm) is the economic system the Colonies lived under. It benefited England at the expense of the Colonies.

unalienable (un-AYE-lee-un-uh-bul) means, in the Declaration of Independence, rights that can't be denied anyone because people are born with them. Sometimes this word is "inalienable." It means the same thing.

spectral (SPEK-truhl) means ghost-like.

ingest (in-JEST) means to eat something.

nomadic (noh-MAD-ick) comes from the word "nomad," which means a wanderer. Nomadic tribes travel from place to place for their livelihood.

abolish (uh-BAHL-ish) means to destroy.

despotism (DES-puh-tiz-uhm) is a kind of government in which the ruler has absolute power. The ruler who has all the power is called a despot (DES-puht).

usurp (you-SURP) means to use wrongfully or to take authority that isn't really yours.

circa (SIR-cuh) means about or in the time of. It is almost always associated with a date. Sometimes it's abbreviated like this: c. 450 B.C.

celestial (suh-LESS-chull) has to do with the sky but suggests something heavenly.

terrestrial (tuhr-RES-tree-uhl) refers to the Earth.

LEARN THE WORDS

Subject Matter Review

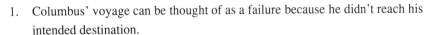

1. Columbus' voyage can be thought of as a failure because he didn't reach his intended destination.
2. The American Indians at the time of Columbus were the descendants of nomadic tribes that crossed in to the New World from Asia.
3. European ideas of what the native Americans were like were greatly distorted by reports brought back by early explorers.
4. Puritans settling the Massachusetts Bay Colony for religious reasons governed themselves with less tolerance than had the English from whom they had fled.
5. The English thought the only reasons for their American colonies to exist were to provide raw materials for British industry and to serve as a market for manufactured goods.
6. The colonies were successful in the revolution because:
   A. They used tactics they had learned from the Indians.
   B. They had much help from England's European rivals.
   C. The British supply line was so long.
   D. Britain was weakened by a long series of wars with European neighbors.
   E. The English people and many government officials tired of the war.
7. The Revolutionary War was the longest U.S. war until Vietnam.
8. After much debate, the framers of our Constitution developed the system we use today. It calls for strict checks and balances among the three branches of government: judicial (Supreme Court and other federal courts), executive (President), and legislative (Congress).

LEARN THE FACTS

In this and the other Social Studies programs, you will often hear "-cracy" words. "-cracy" is a word part that refers to government.

demo ("people")
+ cracy ("government")
_____

= democracy ("government by the people")

List other "-cracy" words.

_____
_____
_____
_____
_____
_____
_____

LEARN THE SKILLS

Don't confuse these two prefixes: <u>anti-</u> and <u>ante-</u>. <u>Anti-</u> means "against":
<u>anti-slavery</u> means "against slavery." <u>Ante-</u> means "before": ante ("before") +
bellum ("war") means "before the war." In the United States, <u>antebellum</u> refers
specifically to the time before the Civil War.

Study this map and answer the questions.

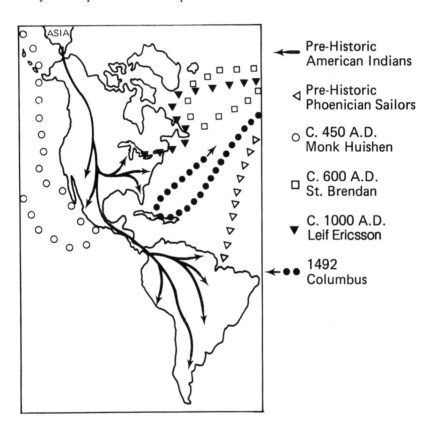

PRACTICE
THE SKILLS

Select the best answers to the questions using information found on the map.

1. Which of the following would be the best   1. ① ② ③ ④ ⑤
   title for this map?
   1) North America Then and Now
   2) Columbus' First Voyage
   3) Who Discovered America?
   4) North and South America
   5) Where the Indians Lived

Subject Matter Review (continued)

2. From the information on the map, which of the following is the most likely origin of Monk Huishen?
   1) Africa
   2) Europe
   3) South America
   4) present-day Canada
   5) Asia

2.① ② ③ ④ ⑤

3. If the map is correct about the route of the American Indians, it would tend to support the theory that says
   1) the Earth is round.
   2) Asia and North America were once connected by a "land bridge."
   3) there is really only one ocean in the world, since all of them are connected to each other.
   4) South America and Africa were once the same land mass.
   5) the Indians came to this continent in search of food.

3.① ② ③ ④ ⑤

Answers:
1. 3   2. 5   3. 2

CHECK YOUR ANSWERS

PRACTICE THE SKILLS

Read this famous poem. It was written to celebrate the Centennial of our country.

CONCORD HYMN
Ralph Waldo Emerson (1803-1882)

Sung at the completion of the Battle Monument, July 4, 1837

I.   By the rude bridge that arched the flood,
          Their flag to April's breeze unfurled,
       Here once the embattled farmers stood
          And fired the shot heard round the world.

II.   The foe long since in silence slept;
        Alike the conqueror silent sleeps;
And Time the ruined bridge has swept
        Down the dark stream which seaward creeps.

III.   On this green bank, by this soft stream,
        We set today a votive stone;
That memory may their deed redeem,
        When, like our sire, our sons are gone.

IV.   Spirit, that made those heroes dare,
        To die, and leave their children free,
Bid Time and Nature gently spare
        The shaft we raise to them and thee.

Now answer these questions.

1. The last two lines of the first stanza are familiar to all of us. Emerson chose the figure of speech "and fired the shot heard round the world" to describe the first shot of the Revolution because
   1) it was very loud.
   2) the Revolution started there.
   3) it's poetic.
   4) the Revolution had worldwide implications.
   5) none of the above

1. ① ② ③ ④ ⑤

2. In stanza II, what does he say happened to the bridge?
   1) It washed away.
   2) It was worn out.
   3) No one knows its location.
   4) both 1) and 2)
   5) none of the above

2. ① ② ③ ④ ⑤

3. In stanza III, the "votive stone" refers to the
   1) rocky shore of the stream
   2) U.S.
   3) stone fences
   4) Battle Monument
   5) stone bridge

3. ① ② ③ ④ ⑤

**CHECK YOUR
ANSWERS**

**PRACTICE
THE SKILLS**

**Subject
Matter
Review**
(continued)

Answers:
1. 4   2. 4   3. 4

As you read materials from the social studies, you will need to use all the reading skills we have been talking about in this series. Let's take a moment to review some of the most important ones.

Using Context Clues

In the exercise below, we've underlined the words we think may be unfamiliar to you. Read the passage and answer the questions.

<u>Ethnologists</u> studying native American cultures
     (1)
estimate that at the time of Columbus' arrival there

were more than one million <u>indigenous</u> people living
          (2)
in that part of the world that was to become the

<u>contiguous</u> United States.
   (3)
  This number declined steadily through war, disease,

and deliberate <u>extermination</u>. By 1890, only 90,000
      (4)
native Americans remained. In many ways, the

<u>philosophies</u> of the native Americans were <u>diametrically</u>
   (5)   (6)
opposed to those of the Europeans.

  Despite their opinion that the Indians were uncivilized,

the colonists borrowed heavily of the native culture.

  For example: Benjamin Franklin recognized the legal

wisdom in the "Law of the Great Peace of the Iroquois."

  As a result, this law became the <u>precursor</u> for the Articles
             (7)
of Confederation and, later, the Constitution.

Look back at each numbered word in the passage, then choose the word that best matches it.

1. 1) cultural scientists
    2) workmen
    3) students
    4) natural scientists
    5) travelers

    1. ① ② ③ ④ ⑤

2. 1) Indian
    2) native
    3) European
    4) savage
    5) foreign

    2. ① ② ③ ④ ⑤

3. 1) original
    2) touching
    3) colonial
    4) New England
    5) fifty

    3. ① ② ③ ④ ⑤

4. 1) assistance
    2) genocide
    3) support
    4) protection
    5) aid

    4. ① ② ③ ④ ⑤

5. 1) practices
    2) ideas
    3) homes
    4) lives
    5) stories

    5. ① ② ③ ④ ⑤

6. 1) differently
    2) similarly
    3) completely
    4) slightly
    5) almost

    6. ① ② ③ ④ ⑤

Subject
Matter
Review
(continued)

7. 1) style
    2) antithesis
    3) law
    4) appendix
    5) forerunner

7. ① ② ③ ④ ⑤

Answers:

1. 1	2. 2	3. 2	4. 2
5. 2	6. 3	7. 5	

**CHECK YOUR
ANSWERS**

Betsy Ross didn't come into our folklore as the designer of the first American flag until nearly 100 years after the incident is supposed to have occurred.

Philadelphia was preparing for its centennial celebration when Betsy's grandson, William Canby, told the Philadelphia Historical Society in 1870 that his grandmother had told him the story when he was a boy. Apparently, the Society was so pleased to have found a local heroine that no one bothered to check out the story. There is no official record that Betsy ever made flags for anyone except the Pennsylvania navy.

Knowing whether Betsy made the original Stars and Stripes may not be as important as wondering how much of our known history has so little basis in fact.

**PRACTICE
THE SKILLS**

Determining the Main Idea

1. Which is the best title for this passage?
    1) The Stars and Stripes
    2) Betsy Ross an Imposter?
    3) Betsy Ross' Grandson Tells It All
    4) Betsy Ross Didn't Design Our Flag After All
    5) William Canby's Grandmother

1. ① ② ③ ④ ⑤

Drawing a Conclusion

2. ① ② ③ ④ ⑤

2. From this same article, you could conclude
   1) Betsy Ross absolutely didn't design the flag.
   2) the author believes that other events haven't been reported accurately.
   3) it happened so long ago that it doesn't make any difference.
   4) all the things we believe about Betsy Ross are untrue.
   5) there isn't enough information to be sure.

Evaluating Fact or Opinion

3. ① ② ③ ④ ⑤

3. According to the article,
   1) William Canby told the truth about his grandmother.
   2) the Historical Society did the right thing in honoring Betsy Ross.
   3) the author of the passage told the correct version.
   4) Pennsylvania had its own navy until 1870.
   5) There isn't enough information given to be sure about any of the above.

Answers:
1. 2   2. 2   3. 5

CHECK YOUR ANSWERS

Just for Fun

Do you think the 12th president of the United States was Zachary Taylor? Most people do. Listen to this strange set of circumstances before you decide.

James Polk, the 11th president, ended his term of office on March 3, 1849, which was a Saturday. At midnight Zachary Taylor should have been president, but he was a devout Episcopalian and refused to celebrate the inauguration until Monday, March 5. For this 24-hour period, our country had no *elected* president. Because the president was not sworn in, neither was Millard Fillmore, the newly elected vice president.

Subject Matter Review (continued)

The law governing succession to the presidency called for the president pro tempore of the senate to automatically be president in the absence of a president and vice-president. By this reasoning, David Rice Atchison, president pro tempore of the senate, was president for a day.

When asked about it, Atchison said he had been overly tired from senate business and slept most of the day, his entire term of office.

By another set of odd circumstances, Atchison was also the unofficial vice president.

Test-Taking Tip

Sometimes you are asked to choose the best answer from among several choices. "Best" means *of those items listed*. You may in fact know a better answer; but if it isn't on the list, it doesn't count.

> **Who was the most influential leader of the "Committees of Correspondence"?**
> 1) **Samuel Adams**
> 2) **Sir Walter Raleigh**
> 3) **John White**
> 4) **Sir Edmund Andros**
> 5) **King George**

The answer to this question is 1. Adams probably *was* the most influential, but it's really a matter of opinion. However, none of the others listed had anything whatever to do with the Committees of Correspondence. Therefore, *of those listed*, Adams was certainly the most influential.

Read this article and answer the questions.

EXTRA PRACTICE

Ten Famous Women of Our Early History

Here's a little sociological research you can do, and it won't take more than 10 minutes to prove a point.

Ask five people to name 10 famous women who lived between 1600 and 1800.

If the five people came up with a *total* of seven *different* names, you've been talking to five exceptionally well informed people.

You'll probably get Virginia Dare, Priscilla Alden, Pocahontas, Martha Washington, and Betsy Ross for starters. You might get Anne Hutchison and Molly Pitcher. It's possible, though unlikely, that someone will know that Molly Pitcher's real name was Mary Ludwig Hays.

Only scholars will know Lydia Darrogh, who spied for Washington, and Deborah Sampson, who dressed as a man so she could serve in the military.

Subject
Matter
Review
(continued)

The law of averages would suggest that something is wrong. Most people could list dozens of men of those centuries who have distinguished themselves.

But check our list again. Historical oversight would be a charitable explanation, but prejudice would be more accurate.

Now answer these questions.

1. The author of this passage believes that women
   1) haven't accomplished many great things.
   2) accomplished great things but didn't tell anyone about them.
   3) were accidentally left out of the history books.
   4) were intentionally left out of a place in history.
   5) none of the above

   1. ① ② ③ ④ ⑤

2. This article is mainly about
   1) history
   2) famous women in American history
   3) the way women have been treated unfairly in history
   4) famous women five people can list
   5) none of the above

   2. ① ② ③ ④ ⑤

3. Only *nine* women are listed in this article because
   1) the author could only think of nine.
   2) there *are* only nine famous women of that period.
   3) omitting one name from a list of 10 demonstrates the purpose of the article.
   4) the history books are so full of the names of famous women the author didn't know which to choose.
   5) It isn't possible to infer what the author might think.

   3. ① ② ③ ④ ⑤

Answers:
   1. 4   2. 3   3. 3

CHECK YOUR
ANSWERS

Chapter
Thirteen
Social
Studies

This program opens with George Washington serving as president of the brand new country, the United States of America. The capital is in New York, but a new seat of government is being imagined, planned, and surveyed.

Pay attention to the different political philosophies of the day. Many of the conflicts and questions that arose at this time are still being talked about today.

Notice particularly the power and excitement of an expanding new nation. Keep in mind the adventure as the people moved westward through the Cumberland Gap. Be alert to the problems caused by each new experience. What were the solutions?

This program takes us from the post-revolution era, when the main concern was establishing a government for a few states along the Atlantic coast, to a time when the country extended to the Pacific.

One of the hard questions to answer about this part of our history is implied in this program. It may not be as easy to answer as you think. As you watch the video, ask yourself, "Who were the heroes?"

Goal-Setting Exercise for Program 13

Read this excerpt from the video and answer the questions.

> **On inauguration day, Jefferson wore plain clothes and, rather than ride in a carriage, chose to walk among the common folk. People thought he was showing his sympathy for the common people. Ironically, Jefferson had ordered a new velvet suit and an expensive carriage, but both failed to arrive in time for the inauguration.**

Now answer these questions.

1. Which of the following figures of speech best tells the main idea of this passage?
   1) A bird in the hand is worth two in the bush.
   2) Laugh and the world laughs with you.
   3) Making the best of a bad situation.
   4) Virtue is its own reward.
   5) Pretty is as pretty does.

   1. ① ② ③ ④ ⑤

2. This passage implies that
   1) Jefferson intended to mislead the people.
   2) he walked because he had no choice.
   3) Jefferson started the trend toward simpler inaugurations.
   4) presidents before Jefferson had also walked.
   5) all presidents since Jefferson have walked.

   2. ① ② ③ ④ ⑤

3. Which of the following words could best replace "ironically?"
   1) fortunately
   2) interestingly
   3) hopefully
   4) cautiously
   5) literally

   3. ① ② ③ ④ ⑤

Goal-Setting Exercise for Program 13 (continued)

4. You could assume from the way Jefferson handled the situation that he
    1) would have liked to have had a carriage.
    2) didn't care one way or the other.
    3) was glad it worked out the way it did.
    4) became angry about the whole thing.
    5) was a good politician.

4. ① ② ③ ④ ⑤

Answers for Goal-Setting Exercise:

1. 3   2. 2   3. 2   4. 5

CHECK YOUR
ANSWERS

Viewing Prescription for Program 13

❏ If you got them **all right** … you are doing fine! Concentrate on the main ideas in the program.

❏ If you missed number **1** … are you still having trouble finding the *main idea* when it isn't directly stated? Try to remember exercises used earlier relating to this skill.

❏ If you missed number **2** or **4** … these are *inference* problems. Watch for similar questions in the video and workbook exercises.

❏ If you missed number **3** … review the suggestions on using *context clues* in Chapter Twelve.

206   BEFORE YOU WATCH THE PROGRAM

Vocabulary for Program 13

Federalists These were the people who believed the government should be strong and that it should help business and industry.

Louisiana Purchase Land the U.S. purchased from France during the time of Thomas Jefferson's presidency. Purchasing land was a major way in which our country grew.

spoils system The practice of the party in power of awarding jobs or other benefits to its supporters. "To the victors belong the spoils" is a saying which describes this system.

Manifest Destiny The idea that the United States had not only the right but the duty to expand throughout the North American continent.

oligarchy means "rule by a few."

Carpetbaggers People sent by the federal government to re-establish government in the South after the Civil War. The name came from the suitcases made from carpet which many used.

Scalawags Southerners who sided with the Yankees after the Civil War.

LEARN THE WORDS

Now Watch Program 13

Subject Matter Review

1. The first U.S. capital was New York.
2. The capital was moved to Washington, DC when Thomas Jefferson was president.
3. The current "two-party system" can be traced to the time of Jefferson and Hamilton.
4. Hamilton's major contribution was his financial plan, which is still used in our government.
5. The Louisiana Purchase began a 50-year period of territorial expansion of our country.
6. Westward expansion caused the exploitation of the Indians and their territories.
7. Differences in the economic bases of the North and South in the mid-1800s contributed to the conditions that led the states to war.
8. The early days of the Civil War were costly and indecisive because leaders on both sides had learned and were using the same tactics.
9. Many Southerners cheered the death of Lincoln, but his death created more problems for the South. Lincoln had urged treating Southern states with compassion. The leaders who took over ignored that advice.

LEARN THE FACTS

People are **concrete**. Their beliefs are **abstract**. Below is a list of words in their concrete forms. Fill in the blanks with the abstract forms.

Concrete	Abstract
Federalist	_____
Aristocrat	_____
Abolitionist	_____
Tyrant	_____

PRACTICE THE SKILLS

Answers:
1. Federalism—the belief in a strong federal government.
2. Aristocracy—the belief that the rich should be in charge of the government.
3. Abolitionism—the desire to abolish something, such as slavery.
4. Tyranny—the rule of an all-powerful person or government, usually by force.

CHECK YOUR ANSWERS

Look at this map of our country at the end of the Revolutionary War. Compare it with the map of the middle 19th century.

PRACTICE
THE SKILLS

THE UNITED STATES IN 1783

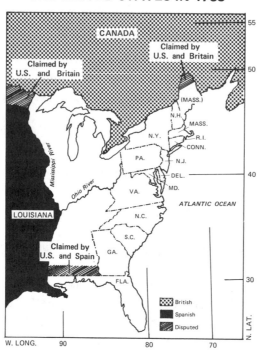

THE UNITED STATES IN 1860

Subject
Matter
Review
(continued)

Now answer these questions about the maps.

1. ① ② ③ ④ ⑤

1. Which of the following countries is *not* shown
   to have holdings in 1783?
   1) Britain
   2) France
   3) Spain
   4) United States
   5) both France and Spain

2. Which of the following was not a state in
   1783?

2. ① ② ③ ④ ⑤

   1) Pennsylvania
   2) Georgia
   3) South Carolina
   4) Maine
   5) Massachusetts

3. According to the 1860 map, which of the following is the most accurate statement?

3. ① ② ③ ④ ⑤

   1) New land acquired after the Revolutionary
       War was very nearly the same size as the
       United States of Washington's time.
   2) Florida originally included part of
       Texas.
   3) The U.S. extended to the Pacific as early
       as 1845.
   4) 1) and 3) but not 2)
   5) 1) and 2) but not 3)

Evaluate this excerpt from the video.

> **Previously, Jefferson believed what the Constitution doesn't
> permit, it forbids; now, with the Louisiana Purchase, he acted like
> Hamilton, who believed what the Constitution doesn't forbid, it
> permits.**

Now answer these questions.

4. It can be inferred from this passage that   4. ① ② ③ ④ ⑤
   1) Hamilton had been right all along.
   2) the two men's ideas weren't so far apart
      after all.
   3) Jefferson had been wrong before.
   4) something made Jefferson change his mind.
   5) None of these possibilities can be in-
      ferred.

5. Jefferson's first idea was   5. ① ② ③ ④ ⑤
   1) much like Hamilton's.
   2) like Washington's.
   3) the opposite of Hamilton's.
   4) like Hamilton's but not like Washing-
      ton's.
   5) unlike both Hamilton's and Washington's.

Answers:
 1. 2   2. 4   3. 1   4. 4   5. 3

**CHECK YOUR
ANSWERS**

Study the map below and compare it to the 1783 map on page 208.

MAP (CIRCA 1850)

1. According to the 1783 map, Spain claimed the   1. ① ② ③ ④ ⑤
   Louisiana Territory in 1783. We bought it
   from France 20 years later. Which of the
   following best explains how that is possible?
   1)   The map is probably wrong.
   2)   France gave the land to Spain.
   3)   Somehow France got the land from Spain.
   4)   We bought Louisiana from Spain.
   5)   France served as an agent for Spain.

2. According to the 1850 map, which of the fol-   2. ① ② ③ ④ ⑤
   lowing cities is closest to 30°N lat. and
   90°W long.?
   1)   Boston
   2)   St. Louis
   3)   New Orleans
   4)   Chicago
   5)   Los Angeles

3. The Oregon Country originally extended north   3. ① ② ③ ④ ⑤
   of the boundary shown on the map. The dis-
   puted location of that boundary inspired a
   famous slogan. Which of the following slogans
   tells about the argument?
   1)   Remember the Maine.
   2)   Remember Pearl Harbor.
   3)   Give me liberty or give me death.
   4)   Remember the Alamo.
   5)   Fifty-four forty or fight.

4. Which of the following tells the approximate   4. ① ② ③ ④ ⑤
   latitude of the southernmost part of Alaska?
   1)   40°N
   2)   55°N
   3)   23°S
   4)   90°N
   5)   170°N

Subject
Matter
Review
(continued)

5. Using information from the maps, which of the   5. ① ② ③ ④ ⑤
   following statements is true?
   1) Alaska is not as big as Texas.
   2) The states west of the Mississippi River
      are generally smaller than the states
      east of the Mississippi.
   3) If the Oregon boundary had been set at
      54° 40', Alaska would have been connected
      to the rest of the states.
   4) Vermont was one of the original states.
   5) West Virginia was established before
      1783.

Answers:

1. 3   2. 3   3. 5   4. 2   5. 3

CHECK YOUR
ANSWERS

PRACTICE
THE SKILLS

The video portion of this program mentioned the "Trail of Tears." Below is a
newspaper article which refers to this time. Read the article and answer the
questions.

THE MUNCIE STAR, SUNDAY, APRIL 8, 1984

Cherokees Let State Keep Sacred Land

By JACK MALTBY
United Press International

RED CLAY, Tenn — The council of the Cherokee Nation, meeting on sacred Indian ground stolen by the white man in the 1830s, voted Saturday to let the state of Tennessee keep the land as a state park.

Chief Robert Youngdeer of the Eastern Band of Cherokees authored a resolution asking the state to return land where the Cherokees held their last council meeting before the "Trail of Tears" march to Oklahoma in 1838.

When the resolution came up for discussion, Youngdeer asked that it be withdrawn, saying he thought the state of Tennessee was doing a good job of memorializing the Cherokees with a state park at Red Clay.

Tennessee lawmakers established Red Clay State Historical Area, a 275-acre park, in 1979 to remember the Cherokee presence in southern Appalachia.

"We have found Red Clay state park to be a beautiful, well-kept, well-respected memorial to our ancestors," Youngdeer told the council. "This state park has lived up to the expectations our ancestors, who lived here 146 years ago, would have for it."

The 27-member council unanimously approved Youngdeer's motion to withdraw the resolution.

Most Cherokees attending the reunion agreed with the council decision to let the state keep Red Clay, but some disagreed.

"Our ancestors had it. We should have it," said Pat Kirkland, 29, a homemaker in the Eastern Band. "Our kids are growing up. We need something to show themn. It would be something special to have it ours."

Joel Queen, a 16-year-old high school student in the Eastern Band, said Red Clay and other special lands should be returned.

"I think all the historical sites should be given back for the Cherokees for them to own and take care of," Queen said.

Chief Ross Swimmer of the Oklahoma Band said leaders of the Eastern Band let their hearts overrule their heads when they proposed getting Red Clay back in the hands of the tribe.

"The emotion of the times probably overcame some people and they said, 'Why don't we ask for Red Clay back?' But after looking at it more closely they saw it wasn't practical," said Swimmer, a lawyer and banker in Tahlequah, Okla.

Swimmer said the tribe would be wise to let the state continue paying the annual $32,000 cost of maintaining the state park, located on the Tennessee-Georgia border.

"The economics of it aren't good. There are a lot of costs associated with it. We'd have to charge fees to visitors. It's just not practical for the tribe to operate it," Swimmer said.

About 20,000 people, including a few thousand Cherokees, jammed the park Saturday to celebrate the first reunion of the Cherokee Nation since the forced move west. More than 10,000 people attended the first day of the 2-day celebration Friday.

Some 17,000 Cherokees were forced to leave their homeland in the Southeast and walk to what is now Oklahoma in the winter of 1838. One-quarter of the population died along the Trail of Tears.

A small band of Cherokees—no more than 1,200—escaped the forced removal by hiding in the North Carolina mountains. They became the Eastern Band of the tribe.

Before Friday, the elected councils for the two tribes had never met in joint council. They adopted a resolution Saturday calling for annual meetings in the future.

Subject Matter Review (continued)

1. To find out what this article is mainly about, you need to read only paragraph
   1) 4
   2) 1
   3) 6
   4) 7
   5) 11

1. ① ② ③ ④ ⑤

2. Which of the following statements best describes the comparison of the Oklahoma Band with the Eastern Band?
   1) The Oklahoma Band is older.
   2) The Eastern Band is the more militant of the two.
   3) The article implies no basic differences in the ideas held by the different bands.
   4) The Eastern Band is the larger of the two.
   5) Their philosophies are exactly alike.

2. ① ② ③ ④ ⑤

3. The author of this article says the sacred land was "stolen" from the Cherokees. Which of the following would most agree with this choice of words?
   1) the U.S. government of the 1830s
   2) the Eastern Band of Cherokees
   3) Tennessee state park officials
   4) the entire Cherokee Nation
   5) the U.S. Department of the Interior

3. ① ② ③ ④ ⑤

Answers:
   1. 2   2. 2   3. 2

CHECK YOUR
ANSWERS

PRACTICE THE SKILLS

Now read these thumbnail biographies of two of the people who influenced this period of time.

HENRY DAVID THOREAU

He was described by his friend Nathaniel Hawthorne as "wild of nature and ugly as sin." It is true he was part of nature; his famous book, *Walden*, stands to this day as proof.

As he lived *Walden*, by going into the woods and living close to nature, so did he live another work, *Civil Disobedience*. He refused to pay taxes to a government that supported an army and approved of slavery. He followed his belief that "the government that governs best, governs least"—to which he later added, "The best of all government governs not at all." This little bit of activism landed him in jail.

He believed it was the responsibility of citizenship to show disapproval of governmental policy when it was contrary to an individual's interpretation of morality.

1. Thoreau was
   1) ugly as sin
   2) said to be "ugly as sin"
   3) a philosopher, not a "doer"
   4) a criminal
   5) greatly appreciated during his day

1. ① ② ③ ④ ⑤

2. What cause-and-effect relationship is implied in this passage?
   1) Because he was wild, he was ugly as sin.
   2) He lived the concepts of *Walden*.
   3) He didn't pay taxes and was sent to jail.
   4) The government that governs best, governs least.
   5) The responsibility of citizenship is to disobey government policy.

2. ① ② ③ ④ ⑤

3. During the early and middle 1980s, the "Sanctuary Movement" illegally aided South Americans in reaching and staying in the United States. We can infer that, if Thoreau were alive, he would have
   1) strongly disapproved of the movement.
   2) agreed with the movement.
   3) agreed with the movement but not supported it.
   4) applauded the movement and supported it.
   5) There is no way to know for sure.

3. ① ② ③ ④ ⑤

ELI WHITNEY

The lifetime inventive work of Eli Whitney, looking back, can be viewed as a series of mixed blessings.

He is best known for the invention of the cotton gin, which took the hand work out of cleaning the cotton fibers from the plant. The gin gave the South many wealthy plantation owners, but it also increased the South's dependence on a "one-crop economy."

The more modern machinery made slavery less attractive and less profitable. As the cotton fields grew, the soil was depleted of the nutrients necessary to grow cotton. In this sense, Whitney paved the highway that led to the downfall of the South.

After a series of thefts of his machine and arson in his factory, Whitney turned to making rifles for the government. His contribution was not that he could make fine firearms but that he made them all alike, with interchangeable parts. No longer was each musket one of a kind. If a rifle failed, another piece just like the broken one was easily and cheaply available.

The North took up his idea of mass production and became a major industrial force in the world. When the Civil War came, 35 years after Whitney's death, the South could in no way match the industrial strength of the North.

The North was not immune to the "curse" of Whitney inventions. They specialized so heavily in industry that a "sweatshop" economy and accompanying social problems became almost as destructive as the one crop/slavery mix of the Southern economy.

4. This article is mainly about
   1) the inventions of Eli Whitney
   2) the Southern "one-crop" economy
   3) Whitney's troubles
   4) the industrial North
   5) the good and bad effects of the Whitney inventions

4. ① ② ③ ④ ⑤

5. If you were to draw a conclusion, which of the following would you say had the greatest long-term effect on our country?
   1) the invention of the cotton gin
   2) the depletion of Southern soil
   3) Whitney's manufacture of rifles
   4) the impact the cotton gin had on slavery
   5) mass production based on replaceable parts

5. ① ② ③ ④ ⑤

Subject Matter Review (continued)

Answers:

1. 2   2. 3   3. 4   4. 5   5. 5

CHECK YOUR ANSWERS

Just for Fun

1. Which states in our country do not have borders common with any other state?
2. Which state touches only one other state?
3. Which state touches the most other states?
4. Realizing that Canada is our neighbor to the north, what direction do you go from Detroit, Michigan to Windsor, Ontario, Canada?
5. Which four states come together at the same point?

Answers:

1. Alaska and Hawaii
2. Maine
3. Tennessee
4. south
5. New Mexico, Arizona, Colorado, Utah

CHECK YOUR ANSWERS

Test-Taking Tip

When you're faced with a question you don't know the answer to, use the process of elimination to get closer to the correct answer. All you do is disregard the *least* likely answers. The ones remaining have a better chance of being right. Example:

> **In order for the U.S. to extend its borders from the Atlantic to the Pacific Ocean, it was necessary to annex the Oregon Territory or California. Several countries had claims on both territories. California was part of Mexico, though Russia had some claim to it. The British claimed much of the Northwest. The United States claimed a portion of the area because of exploration rights and the Louisiana Purchase from France. The problem was not resolved until after Texas pulled away from Mexico.**
>
> **Which of these countries was *least* likely to be involved in our acquisition of California?**
> 1) **Russia**
> 2) **Mexico**
> 3) **France**
> 4) **Spain**
> 5) **Texas**

The correct answer is 4. The others were all mentioned, so you can conclude that they *may* have had something to do with California.

After the Constitution was ratified, some additions were quickly written. These first 10 amendments are called the Bill of Rights. To change the Constitution today, we still have to write and approve amendments.

So far in this series, we haven't done anything with dictionary skills. Read the Bill of Rights and use a dictionary to find the meanings of words you don't understand. In the space provided, paraphrase each of the amendments.

EXTRA PRACTICE

BILL OF RIGHTS

AMENDMENT I. Freedom of Religion, Speech, and Press; Rights of Assembly and Petition

Congress shall make no law respecting an establishment of religion, or prohibiting the free exercise thereof; or abridging the freedom of speech or of the press; or the right of the people peaceably to assemble, and to petition the government for a redress of grievances.

AMENDMENT II. Right To Bear Arms

A well-regulated militia being necessary to the security of a free State, the right of the people to keep and bear arms shall not be infringed.

AMENDMENT III. Quartering of Troops

No soldier shall, in time of peace, be quartered in any house without the consent of the owner, nor in time of war, but in a manner to be prescribed by law.

AMENDMENT IV. Searches and Seizures

The right of the people to be secure in their persons, houses, papers, and effects, against unreasonable searches and seizures, shall not be violated; and no warrants shall issue but upon probable cause,[1] supported by oath or affirmation, and particularly describing the place to be searched, and the persons or things to be seized.

AMENDMENT V. Rights of Accused Persons; Property Rights

No person shall be held to answer for a capital, or otherwise infamous crime, unless on a presentment or indictment of a grand jury, except in cases arising in the land or naval forces, or in the militia, when in actual service in time of war or public danger; nor shall any person be subject for the same offense to be twice put in jeopardy of life or limb; nor shall be compelled in any criminal case to be a witness against himself; nor be deprived of life, liberty, or property, without due process of law; nor shall private property be taken for public use without just compensation.

AMENDMENT VI. Additional Rights of Accused Persons

In all criminal prosecutions, the accused shall enjoy the right of a speedy and public trial, by an impartial jury of the State and district wherein the crime shall have been committed, which district shall have been previously ascertained by law; and to be informed of the nature and cause of the accusation; to be confronted with the witnesses against him; to have compulsory process for obtaining witnesses in his favor,[2] and to have the assistance of counsel for his defense.

AMENDMENT VII. Suits at Common Law

In suits at common law,[3] where the value in controversy shall exceed twenty dollars, the right of trial by jury shall be preserved, and no fact tried by a jury shall be otherwise re-examined in any court of the United States, than according to the rules of the common law.

AMENDMENT VIII. Bails, Fines, and Punishments

Excessive bail shall not be required, nor excessive fines imposed, nor cruel and unusual punishment inflicted.

AMENDMENT IX. Rights not Enumerated

The enumeration in the Constitution of certain rights shall not be construed to deny or disparage others retained by the people.

AMENDMENT X. Powers Reserved to the States and to the People

The powers not delegated to the United States by the Constitution, nor prohibited to it by the State, are reserved to the States respectively, or to the people.

[1] "Probable cause" means reasonable grounds of suspicion.
[2] The accused person has the right to request the court to issue an order, or subpoena, compelling a witness to appear in court.
[3] "Common law" is law based on custom and precedent (past decisions). Originating in England, it was brought to America by the settlers. It became the foundation of our legal system.

Write the words you want to remember:

_____

_____

Paraphrased rights:

I. _____

_____

II. _____

_____

III. _____

_____

IV. _____

_____

V. _____

_____

VI. _____

_____

VII. _____

_____

VIII._____

_____

Subject Matter Review (continued)

IX. _____

_____

X. _____

_____

Here is what Thomas Jefferson said about the Bill of Rights.

> **I have a right to nothing which another has a right to take away. And Congress will have a right to take away trial by jury in civil cases. Let me add that a bill of rights is what the people are entitled to against every government on Earth, general or particular, and what no just government should refuse or rest on inference.**

1. This quotation says that Jefferson
   1) strongly supports a statement of rights
   2) doesn't care one way or the other about rights
   3) rejects the whole idea of such a statement
   4) implies support of the concept of the rights amendments
   5) His attitude isn't apparent.

   1. ① ② ③ ④ ⑤

2. "… and what no just government should refuse or rest on inference" means that governments
   1) should not grant such rights
   2) to be fair, must not only grant such rights, but must do so in a way that leaves nothing to chance
   3) have no obligation in the matter
   4) have a choice to grant or not to grant rights
   5) all of the above

   2. ① ② ③ ④ ⑤

Answers:
Your paraphrases will be different from everyone else's.

   1. 1   2. 2

CHECK YOUR ANSWERS

Chapter
Fourteen
Social
Studies

In this lesson, we'll try to apply some of the skills used in the previous lessons. Follow carefully. It may be an entirely new challenge for you.

The title of the video is "Changes—Mass Production, Mass Culture, Mass Conflict." This was truly the era of "the masses."

As you watch, try to put the events of the time into a modern-day perspective. Ask yourself, "How would we deal with this problem today?" or "How would I feel about a similar situation?" or "Have we ever really solved that problem?"

Some of the sequences will tell the story differently from the way you remember it. We want you to form your opinions using what you already know and the new information presented.

This presentation is a showcase of "cause and effect." Be alert to the many situations that point out this element. You also will see historical examples of "means to an end."

This program will test your ability to make inferences. It's an excellent proving ground for your newly sharpened reading skills.

**Goal-
Setting
Exercise
for
Program 14**

Read this selection and answer the questions.

When Woodrow Wilson appointed George Creel to head the Committee on Public Information, our country got its most dedicated appointee.

Creel, a journalist and super patriot to the point of chauvinism, went after his job of selling Wilsonian reform with a zeal unheard of before. He successfully sponsored Liberty Loan bond drives which not only helped finance the war but also made it a part of everyone's commitment. He bombarded the news media with the "information" that best supported Wilson's cause.

To Creel's way of thinking, those who opposed him did so not simply because they were wrong, but because they were *evil*. He appealed to people's emotions by choosing words so carefully that he made his side look good and, at the same time, made his enemies seem less than human.

This quote demonstrates the Creel technique: "I would rather be an American, killed in the unpreparedness that proved devotion is to declared principles, than a German living as the result of years of lying, sneaking, treacherous preparation, for a wolf's spring at the throat of an unsuspecting world."

After he completed his assignment, which lasted less than two years, he might have sunk into relative obscurity and been forgotten if it hadn't been for an Austrian housepainter who, a decade later, picked up Creel's tactics and refined them into the greatest propaganda machine ever known.

The housepainter in question was Adolf Hitler, a person Creel obviously hated.

Now answer these questions.

1. Chauvinism means   1. ① ② ③ ④ ⑤
    1) complete awareness
    2) blind acceptance of a cause
    3) hard-working
    4) unfaithful to an idea
    5) thoughtful, unemotional support of an
        idea

Goal-Setting Exercise for Program 14 (continued)

2. Creel was   2. ① ② ③ ④ ⑤
   1) hard-working
   2) a staunch supporter of President Wilson
   3) extremely patriotic
   4) convinced his ideas were right
   5) all of the above

3. The article implies that George Creel   3. ① ② ③ ④ ⑤
   1) developed the principles of propaganda
   2) didn't know how to work with people
   3) was unhappy with his job
   4) didn't understand politics very well
   5) all of the above

4. You could conclude   4. ① ② ③ ④ ⑤
   1) Creel did many other important things
      after he left office.
   2) Creel's public relations caused others to
      use his ideas.
   3) Adolf Hitler admired Creel as a man.
   4) propaganda is used only in time of war.
   5) all of the above

5. The war mentioned in the passage was   5. ① ② ③ ④ ⑤
   1) the Spanish-American War
   2) World War I
   3) World War II
   4) Vietnam
   5) none of the above

6. From President Wilson's point of view, Creel   6. ① ② ③ ④ ⑤
   1) wasn't to be trusted
   2) was the right man for his job
   3) was unsuccessful
   4) shouldn't have used propaganda
   5) none of the above

Answers for Goal-Setting Exercise:
1. 2   2. 5   3. 1
4. 2   5. 2   6. 2

CHECK YOUR
ANSWERS

Viewing Prescription for Program 14

❏ If you got them **all right** …   keep up the good work! Enjoy the rest of the lesson!

❏ If you missed number **1** …   read the second paragraph again. The definition of <u>chauvinism</u> is there.

❏ If you missed number **2** …   what do you know about Creel's character? Be alert to what the video says about what other historical figures were like.

❏ If you missed number **3** …   watch the video carefully. Many of the ideas discussed still influence our thinking.

❏ If you missed number **4** …   watch for "Big Ideas" which are related to small incidents. The video program is full of them.

❏ If you missed number **5** …   watch the video with *sequence* in mind. Make an outline in your mind of the order in which the events occurred.

❏ If you missed number **6** …   *point of view* is very important in this lesson. The workbook should help you.

Vocabulary for Program 14

plutocracy (plew-TAH-kruh-see) is a government by the wealthy; or the word can refer to a class of rich people who control things. Such a person is called a **plutocrat** (PLEW-tuh-krat).

atrocity (uh-TRAHS-uh-tee) is a brutal or barbaric act.

philanthropy (fill-AN-throw-pee) literally means "love of mankind." It is used to describe someone who does unselfish things for society.

LEARN THE WORDS

Vocabulary for Program 14 (continued)

trust (TRUHST), in this context, means an association of companies organized for defeating competition.

exploitation (eks-ploy-TAY-shun) means to take unfair or destructive advantage of someone or something. The root word is exploit. At various times, humans have been exploited— e.g., as slaves or sweatshop workers.

connotation (kon-oh-TAY-shun) refers to an additional personal meaning beyond what the dictionary says. Example: The word "politician" may mean to you simply someone who works in government or someone who knows how to get other people to do something (like a diplomat). It may have in your mind the connotation of someone who is very undesirable.

propaganda (prah-puh-GAN-duh) refers to the spreading of ideas, rumors, and the like to influence the thinking of a certain population. Propaganda has an unpopular connotation but is not unlike advertising.

isolationism (eye-so-LAY-shun-iz-um) refers to a theory that a government is better off if it doesn't enter into treaties and agreements with other countries.

Prohibition (proh-huh-BISH-uhn) comes from the word prohibit. In this lesson, it refers to a time when alcoholic beverages were prohibited in the United States.

laissez-faire (lay-zay-FARE) is a French term meaning "Let act" (i.e., let things alone). It has come to mean a situation in which those in authority exercise very little or no control.

Treaty of Versailles (TREE-tee) (vair-SIGH) refers to the agreement that ended World War I. Versailles is a city in France.

Now Watch Program 14

1. The early industrial expansion of the U.S. was marked by many forms of exploitation which led, either directly or indirectly, to major changes in our society. Of these changes, the most apparent were
   A. child labor laws
   B. antitrust laws
   C. women's rights
   D. labor movements
2. Interpretation of the Monroe Doctrine led the U.S. to a policy of economic imperialism.
3. The Spanish-American War was a result of this policy.
4. A period of isolationism came to an abrupt end with the beginning of World War I.
5. The economic splurge after World War I ended with the 1929 stock market crash and the following Great Depression.
6. Though no single cause of the Great Depression can be cited, a major contributor was over-speculation, which led to overproduction and wide-spread use of credit, which led to markets based largely on credit.
7. Governmental intervention in the economic ills was only minimally successful.
8. The real cure for the Great Depression came in the form of another war, which provided markets for industry.

LEARN THE FACTS

Here is some more practice in defining words using context clues.

The United States <u>instituted</u> a policy with regard to
(1)
European <u>confrontation</u>. That policy was called
(2)
<u>isolationism</u>—an avoidance of <u>entanglements</u> across
  (3)   (4)
the Atlantic.

This position of <u>neutrality</u>—that is, being neither for
(5)
nor against another nation—began to <u>flag</u> when Archduke
(6)
Ferdinand was killed at <u>Sarajevo</u>. Peace gave way to
(7)
international <u>conflagration</u>.
(8)

PRACTICE THE SKILLS

Subject Matter Review (continued)

Choose the best answers from these responses.

1. 1) schooled
    2) began
    3) evaded
    4) understood
    5) erased

2. 1) conflict
    2) harmony
    3) fellowship
    4) unity
    5) awareness

3. 1) liberalism
    2) capitalism
    3) communism
    4) fascism
    5) non-interference

4. 1) battlegrounds
    2) business
    3) involvements
    4) finance
    5) society

5. 1) indifference
    2) impartiality
    3) detachment
    4) disinterest
    5) all of the above

6. 1) weaken
    2) salute
    3) increase
    4) improve
    5) expand

7. 1) his pajamas
    2) his car
    3) the alley
    4) a telephone booth
    5) a city *someplace*

8. 1) peace
    2) freedom
    3) liberty
    4) calm
    5) war

Answers:

1. 2	2. 1	3. 5	4. 3
5. 2	6. 1	7. 5	8. 5

CHECK YOUR ANSWERS

The following exercises are to help you make connections with your opinions and the ideas expressed in this lesson. Read the selections and respond to the questions.

SELECTION A

In November 1982, two employees of Hitachi, Ltd., the Japanese firm, and Thomas Yoshida, an American citizen, pleaded guilty to a charge of conspiring to steal computer secrets from International Business Machines, Inc.

PRACTICE THE SKILLS

Yoshida was fined $10,000 on a federal charge of conspiring to transport stolen property across state lines.

Hitachi subsequently admitted its part in the espionage and reached an out-of-court settlement, agreeing to pay IBM an estimated $300 million plus $2 million joint court costs.

In addition, IBM received an agreement which allows the firm to inspect future Hitachi products for evidence of patent infringement. If infringement can be proved, Hitachi will not be permitted to distribute the product.

1. Should Hitachi have had to pay IBM for the stolen secrets?
   Yes _____   No _____

2. Do you think most Americans would agree with your answer?
   Yes _____   No _____

3. Do you think the average Japanese would agree with this position?
   Yes _____   No _____

4. How do you feel about the actions of Thomas Yoshida?
   Positive _____   Negative _____
   Neutral _____

5. How do you feel about the actions of Samuel Slater (he was mentioned in the TV program)?
   Positive _____   Negative _____
   Neutral _____

Read this excerpt from the *People's Almanac* and answer the questions.

SELECTION B

WHO REALLY RULES (The United States) There are many forces at work in U.S. society, but the most powerful by far are the interlocking directorates of the major banks, corporations, and insurance companies, with the backing of the military: in the words of former President Dwight Eisenhower, "the military-industrial complex."

Subject Matter Review
(continued)

6. How is this situation the same as it was in the 1900s?

_____

_____

7. How is it different?

_____

_____

Go back to the first page of this lesson and re-read the passage about George Creel; then answer the question below.

SELECTION C

8. Make a list of the "emotion-packed" words in the quotation from George Creel.

_____

_____

SELECTION D

The New Woman

9. What forces in our society inspired this cartoon?

_____

_____

_____

10. In what way does the picture have anything to do with George Creel?

_____
_____
_____

Below is another quote from the video. Read it and respond to the thought questions.

SELECTION E

Contrary to what some history books and a lot of Hollywood movies tell us about "savage" Indians, they were not the only ones committing atrocities. Massacres occurred on both sides as the battle for territory raged during the 19th century.

Indians not killed in battle faced another kind of extermination—by starvation—when their hunting grounds were taken over.

11. What is the difference in meaning between the words "massacre" and "battle"?

_____
_____
_____

12. What are the elements of propaganda in this passage?

_____
_____
_____

Below is an excerpt from the book *The Hidden Persuaders* by Vance Packard. How does this relate to the above quote from the video?

SELECTION F

Perhaps the most spectacularly successful image building has been done by the automobile industry. The automobile has become far more than a mere means of conveyance. In the words of Pierre Mortineau, "The automobile tells who we are and what we think we want to be.... It is a portable symbol of our personality and our position. [In buying a car] you are saying in a sense, 'I am looking for the car that expresses who I am.'"

Subject Matter Review (continued)

13. What conclusions can you draw from this passage that would make you think of the similarities between advertising and propaganda?

_____

_____

_____

14. How can you make a case for the statement, "Advertising was one of the major causes of the Great Depression"?

_____

_____

_____

There are many answers to the thought questions you have just responded to. What details presented support your point of view? There is no way we can check your answers on this exercise. You might want to discuss your answers with a friend or teacher.

Just for Fun

Here's a word search puzzle with a difference. It's based on "word pairs" you heard in the video. The words go together; in the puzzle, they cross each other. The words may be horizontal, vertical, diagonal, or even backward.

Here are the pairs you should be able to find:

Woodrow Wilson	
Great Depression	
Brain Trust	
Grover Cleveland	
New Deal	
Trust Busting	
Laissez-Faire	
Monroe Doctrine	
William Taft	
Wright Brothers	
Big Stick	
Henry Ford	
Good luck!	

```
R U H E R B E R T L C M T S
N O O W V E T B R A I N S H
Y L O I C T O B U S T I N G
I A V L D E M P S T R G I M
H Z E L S D O C T R I N E L
F S R I E S N F T N D E A L
J T T A F T R O P W U W D V
B I G M R R O Y T H E N R Y
I C C L E V E L A N D O O U
P K O V T T S U H F H S F T
B R O T H E R S N A T L O L
C R C G O O R N E I A I A N
G A I S S W O O D R O W D Z
E R M T L A I S S E Z K U S
W D E P R E S S I O N V L S
I A I A E T E E C M B H P A
D O R M T V D R E L X I A T
```

Subject
Matter
Review
(continued)

Test-Taking Tip

Beware of qualifiers! Answers on a test that include <u>all</u>, <u>never</u>, <u>always</u>, or <u>none</u> are usually wrong. Few things "never" or "always" happen. Example:

> **Federal income tax is a recent invention of our government. It wasn't until the 16th Amendment, ratified in 1913, that Congress was authorized to tax individual income.**
>
> **According to this passage,**
> 1) **after 1913, all income was taxed**
> 2) **before 1913, no income was taxed**
> 3) **corporate income has always been taxed**
> 4) **before 1913, none of the money used to run the government came from taxes**
> 5) **the 16th Amendment authorized income taxation**

Answer 5 is the only answer that doesn't contain an "absolute" such as <u>always</u>, <u>none</u>, <u>all</u>, or <u>no</u>. The others do, and they are wrong.

Test designers soften the absolutes with such words as <u>sometimes</u>, <u>seldom</u>, <u>tend to be</u>, and so forth. If you're down to a choice between two answers, see whether one contains an absolute. (It's probably wrong.) If one of them is "softened," there's a good chance it's right.

Read this selection and answer the questions.

Customer No. 1:	**I like Fluff-Fluff much more than the leading brand.**
Customer No. 2:	**Fluff-Fluff is marvelous at combatting static cling.**
Customer No. 3:	**Since I found Fluff-Fluff, my husband's disposition has improved 100%.**

EXTRA PRACTICE

1. From the passage above, it *cannot* be concluded that
   1) Fluff-Fluff is a laundry product
   2) the "leading brand" costs more than Fluff-Fluff
   3) the Fluff-Fluff company interviewed satisfied customers
   4) Fluff-Fluff is not the leading brand
   5) 1) and 3)

1. ① ② ③ ④ ⑤

Subject Matter Review (continued)

2. "Objectivity" means looking at the facts without being influenced by emotion. An example of objectivity is
   1) I like Fluff-Fluff much more than the leading brand.
   2) Fluff-Fluff is marvelous at combatting static cling.
   3) Since I found Fluff-Fluff, my husband's disposition has improved 100%.
   4) 1) and 2) but not 3)
   5) none of the above

2. ① ② ③ ④ ⑤

3. Which of the following is a more objective statement about Fluff-Fluff than any of the above?
   1) Independant laboratory comparison tests show Fluff-Fluff to be a superior product in six of the ten catagories tested.
   2) Sudsy Wash is a crummy product. Fluff-Fluff is much better.
   3) Fluff-Fluff sales have increased 6% yearly for the last 3 years.
   4) 1) and 2) but not 3)
   5) 1) and 3) but not 2)

3. ① ② ③ ④ ⑤

4. Propaganda cannot be *objective*. What Customer No. 3 said is propaganda because it
   1) suggests that all the other products were so bad that they made her husband angry
   2) makes you think Fluff-Fluff will make your husband feel better, too
   3) implies that a woman's main goal in life is to please her husband
   4) makes you think the husband's disposition is 100% improved because Fluff-Fluff is 100% improved
   5) all of the above

4. ① ② ③ ④ ⑤

Answers:
  1. 2   2. 5   3. 5   4. 5

CHECK YOUR ANSWERS

Chapter
Fifteen
Social
Studies

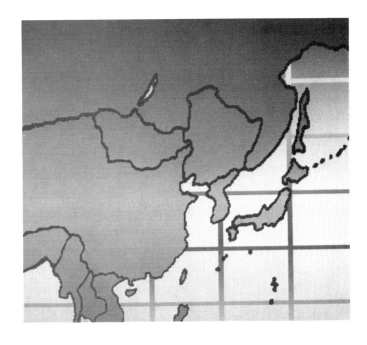

This program begins with the re-establishment of power and politics in Europe. You will see how the ingredients for global conflict resulted in the most violent and destructive period the world has ever known.

Be especially aware of the alliances formed at this time. These were the beginnings of the world political climate as it exists today.

This was a time of extremes. Excitement was balanced with great agony. Germany, for instance, experienced the exhilaration and thrill of a new promise of greatness following the humiliation of World War I. Then this promise was smashed.

In the Far East, Japan was striving to improve almost every part of the lives of its people. Their hopes for expansion and a brighter future were crushed under the horror of a "new" kind of warfare.

Places no one ever heard of before became headline news—places like Alamogordo, Hiroshima, Nagasaki, Korea, and finally Vietnam.

**Goal-
Setting
Exercise
for
Program 15**

Read this selection and answer the questions.

After World War I, Germany was forbidden to engage in any activity remotely resembling militarism. After all, wasn't WWI the war to end all wars?

Sport was exempt from treaty regulations. Universities calmly returned to the medieval custom of dueling. No one could be elected president of a fraternity unless he proudly wore a sabre scar. True to German derring-do, Bavarian skies were soon filled with a new kind of sport glider, so aerodynamically sound that it could ride the air currents thousands of feet into the air. Motors were outlawed, but not the sleek sports planes.

Surely, no one could fault a country for wanting to improve its transportation system. The Autobahn soon became the envy of Europe, as did the German railroads.

It is not that the German people set out to violate the precepts of the treaties. It was only when Hitler, who followed no rules, came along that the fraternity men became army officers, the soaring planes provided the design for the Luftwaffe, and Sunday afternoon aeronauts were instant pilots. The Autobahn and railroads could move troops with astonishing efficiency.

1. According to this article, the German people   1. ① ② ③ ④ ⑤
   1) didn't initially violate the treaty
      agreements
   2) engaged in those things the treaty al-
      lowed
   3) developed great skill in soaring
   4) developed fine highway and rail systems
   5) all of the above

2. The tone of this article suggests that the   2. ① ② ③ ④ ⑤
   author
   1) has high regard for German ingenuity
   2) doesn't care too much for Hitler
   3) thinks dueling is a good idea
   4) all of the above
   5) 1) and 2) but not 3)

Goal-Setting Exercise for Program 15 (continued)

3. Which of the following is *not* a definition of "precepts"?
   1) rules
   2) regulations
   3) mandates
   4) understandings
   5) laws

   3. ① ② ③ ④ ⑤

4. American propaganda during WWII often pictured a German soldier with a scar on his cheek. The reason for this was
   1) it made Germans seem barbaric
   2) to tell Americans that German officers were college men
   3) it was an easy photograph to get
   4) Americans like to see pictures of scars
   5) none of the above

   4. ① ② ③ ④ ⑤

5. To the German soldier, the scar represented
   1) a badge of courage
   2) the result of youthful exuberance
   3) a long-standing tradition among German intellectuals
   4) a sense of belonging with other duelers
   5) all of the above

   5. ① ② ③ ④ ⑤

6. Arthur Kinn says, "You'd best be careful how hard you beat when you beat someone down. It makes them hard to deal with when they get up." This statement
   1) sums up the result of the rigid treaty agreements
   2) disagrees with the main idea of the passage
   3) has nothing whatever to do with the passage
   4) can't be applied to the Germans during WWII
   5) has more to do with street fighting than international politics

   6. ① ② ③ ④ ⑤

Goal-Setting Exercise for Program 15 (continued)

Answers for Goal-Setting Exercise:

1. 5	2. 5	3. 4
4. 1	5. 5	6. 1

CHECK YOUR ANSWERS

Viewing Prescription for Program 15

❑ If you got them **all right** …   wunderbar! Enjoy the program.

❑ If you missed number **1** …   look for the "big ideas" in the program. Some will be directly stated; some will not.

❑ If you missed number **2** …   as you watch the video, pay attention to the *motives* and *attitudes* expressed.

❑ If you missed number **3** …   be alert to how familiar words change meaning when they are used in different ways.

❑ If you missed number **4** …   ask yourself how you feel about the events in this program. It's emotion-packed.

❑ If you missed number **5** …   you need to be alert to how other people feel, as well as to your own emotions.

❑ If you missed number **6** …   sometimes, when you compare two ideas, neither is directly stated. Watch for examples like this one in the video.

Vocabulary for Program 15

Many of these words and terms refer to types of governments or political arrangements. They are abstract; none of the "isms" exists anywhere in pure form.

socialism (SO-shuh-liz-uhm) a government which owns, or holds control of, property and production. The word "Nazi" is short for National Socialism. While there were socialistic (so-shuh-LIS-tick) elements in the Nazi government, it was really a dictatorship.

capitalism (KAP-it-uhl-iz-uhm) is an economic system that allows private ownership of business and property. Decisions are made by individual owners rather than by government. The U.S. is said to be a capitalistic country.

fascism (FASH-iz-uhm) is more a style of government than a form of government. Fascist (FASH-ist) governments are characterized by the oppressive use of force against their own people.

dictatorship (dick-TAY-tuhr-ship) is a form of government in which the leader has *absolute* control. In most cases, the dictator is expected to rule for life. In practice, however, dictators rule until another person or group can get enough power to throw them out and take over.

blitzkreig (BLITZ-kreeg) means "lightning war." It usually refers to the style of attack mounted by WWII German armies.

Luftwaffe (LOOFT-vahf-eh) was the German air force.

kamikaze (kahm-uh-KAH-zee) was a tactic used by the Japanese in which planes were filled with explosives and crashed into the target. They are sometimes called "suicide planes," because the fliers knew they would die when the planes crashed.

coordinates (koh-ORD-in-uhts), as used in this chapter, means the intersection of locator lines on a map. We will be talking about the latitude and longitude of several places.

lethal (LEE-thuhl) means deadly.

LEARN THE WORDS

Subject Matter Review

1. World War II started long before the United States became involved.
2. In Germany, the Nazi government was oppressive and brutal.
3. Japan's sneak attack on Pearl Harbor caused the United States to enter the war.
4. D-Day, the landing of Allied forces on the European continent, was the largest amphibious operation in history.
5. Hitler committed suicide as Allied forces advanced on Berlin.
6. VE-Day signified the end of the European conflict. This was May 7, 1945.
7. The "Island Hopping War" had broken the Japanese hold on the Pacific by VE-Day, but the Japanese didn't surrender because they wanted to maintain their Emperor.
8. Atomic bombs dropped on Hiroshima and Nagasaki killed thousands of Japanese. This attack has long been criticized as unnecessary since the Japanese were about ready to surrender anyway. The action is, however, credited for saving many American lives.
9. Atomic warfare changed our ideas of how war is waged.
10. After the war, U.S. industrial might turned to making consumer goods in greater volume than ever before.
11. The "Cold War" replaced the "Shooting War" as the communist countries aligned.

LEARN THE FACTS

Here is a chronology of the major events during the time covered in the video.

1939   Hitler's Germany invaded Poland and the Low Countries.
1940   Italy invaded Ethiopia.
1941   The Japanese bombed Pearl Harbor; America entered the war.
1944   The Allies invaded Europe.
1945   Roosevelt died; the first atomic bomb was dropped; World War II ended.
1949   Russia exploded its first atomic device, and the Cold War began.
1950   Korean War started.
1953   Korean War ended.
1954   McCarthy was censured by the U.S. Senate.
1955   Rosa Parks refused to give up her seat on a bus.
1956   Egypt seized the Suez Canal.
1957   *Sputnik* sparked the space race.

We worked on map skills in chapter five. Here's a refresher. If you need more help, go back to see what you did there.

LATITUDE refers to the lines that circle the Earth parallel to the equator. It is measured in degrees, minutes, and seconds. LONGITUDE is also measured in degrees, minutes, and seconds. It is computed from the zero point at Greenwich, England and goes both east and west 180 degrees. The big difference between the two is that 0 latitude (the equator) goes completely around the world, while 0 longitude extends only from pole to pole. The extension of this line on the other side of the globe is longitude 180 degrees (east *and* west).

Using this map, list the map coordinates for the countries listed. (Use the coordinate reading for the position of the circle next to each country's name.)

PRACTICE
THE SKILLS

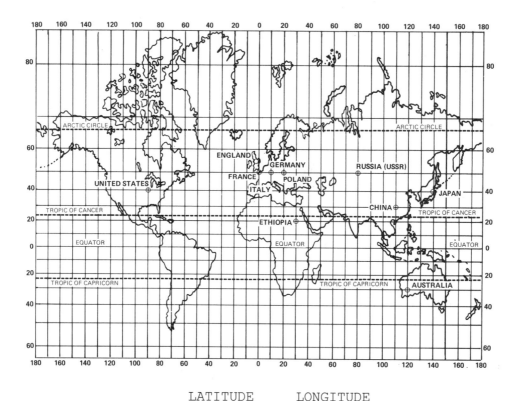

	LATITUDE	LONGITUDE
Example: U.S.A.	*N 40*	*W 90*
1. Ethiopia	_____	_____
2. Italy	_____	_____
3. Poland	_____	_____
4. France	_____	_____
5. Germany	_____	_____
6. Russia	_____	_____
7. England	_____	_____
8. Japan	_____	_____
9. China	_____	_____
10. Australia	_____	_____

Subject Matter Review (continued)

Answers:
1. N20,E30
2. N42, E15 (This one is a little difficult because the circle doesn't fall directly on a crossing of the lines. In that case, you have to estimate.)
3. N50, E20
4. N50, 0 (Zero is neither east nor west.)
5. N50, E10
6. N50, E80
7. N55, 0
8. N40, E140
9. N30, E110
10. S30, E120

CHECK YOUR ANSWERS

Below are some excerpts from the video. Read them just as if you were going to answer questions about them. This time, however, we've listed some responses and starred the "correct" one. Your job is to invent a question for which the answer would be the *best* one.

PRACTICE THE SKILLS

Several aggressive, ruthless rulers were on the world stage by 1940. Benito Mussolini, dictator of Italy, had sent his Fascist army into northern Africa and overrun helpless Ethiopia.

In the Far East, the Japanese army, led by Hideki Tojo, was trying to steal part of China to provide more real estate for Japan's swelling population.

1. _____
   _____
   _____
   _____
   _____

   1) Ethiopia
* 2) Japan
   3) Belgium
   4) Italy
   5) China

The most murderous of all was a former housepainter from Austria, Adolf Hitler. Back in 1924, Hitler had written a book called *Mein Kampf*—"My Struggle"—in which he had laid out his plan to take over Germany and restore it to its role as the world power.

In *Mein Kampf* he told of the "Big Lie" technique.

2. _____
   _____
   _____
   _____
   _____

1) "Big Lie"
2) "World Power"
* 3) "My Struggle"
4) "Adolf Hitler"
5) "Austrian Housepainter"

Hitler thought the Jews were secretly trying to rule and that they must be exterminated so the "superior" Aryan race—the blonde-haired, blue-eyed Germans—could rule instead.

His big lie worked. Most Germans went along with his murderous plan, which he called the "Final Solution." Hitler's countrymen slaughtered six million Jewish men, women, and children, many in specially built showers into which prisoners were herded and showered with not water but lethal gas; mounds of corpses were burned in specially designed ovens.

3. _____
    _____
    _____
    _____
    _____

* 1) trying to take over Germany
2) the superior Aryan race
3) the final solution
4) in need of showers
5) not religious

In no time, our country produced a "baby boom." During the war years and the Depression before it, marriages were postponed and few children were born. But beginning in 1947, the birth rate skyrocketed, and it didn't slow down until the '60s. Women, who'd kept factories and offices running while the men were overseas, gave up their jobs and returned to full-time child rearing. Congress funded the G.I. Bill, which gave men who'd served in the armed forces money to buy homes and go to college.

4. _____
    _____
    _____
    _____
    _____

1) an upsurge in enrollment in the schools in the early '50s
2) an increase in the size of the work force
3) Many veterans went to college.
4) Real estate business improved.
* 5) all of the above

5. _____
_____
_____
_____
_____
_____

   1) remained the same
   2) was like a celebration
   3) decreased significantly
   4) was colorful
* 5) increased rapidly

McCarthy's name became part of our political jargon. "McCarthyism" stands for unwarranted fear and accusations which lead to invasions of privacy and seriously threaten such civil liberties as freedom of speech.

6. _____
_____
_____
_____
_____

   1) policy
   2) invasion of privacy
* 3) specialized language
   4) civil liberties
   5) party

7. _____
_____
_____
_____
_____

   1) political jargon—freedom of speech
   2) "McCarthyism"—jargon
   3) civil liberties—freedom of speech
* 4) accusation—invasion of privacy
   5) none of the above

Subject Matter Review (continued)

Answers:

It's impossible to guess how you phrased each of your questions above. We can tell you how we would have asked the question to get the desired response.

1. Hideki Tojo was the leader of the army of
2. The translation of the title of the book *Mein Kampf* is
3. Hitler thought the Jews were
4. Which of the following resulted from the "baby boom"?
5. The word "skyrocketed" means
6. What does the word "jargon" mean?
7. Which of these pairs explains the cause-and-effect relationship mentioned in the passage?

CHECK YOUR ANSWERS

Below are a graph and a chart. Follow the same procedure as before. Study the information and make up questions that will give the responses we have starred.

PRACTICE THE SKILLS

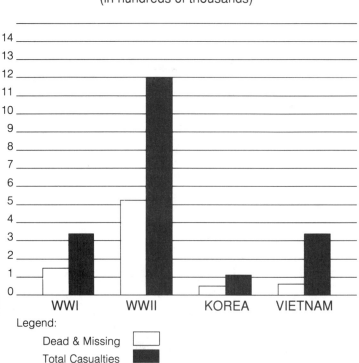

CASUALTIES IN U.S. WARS OF THE 20TH CENTURY
(in hundreds of thousands)

Legend:
Dead & Missing ☐
Total Casualties ■

1. _____
_____
_____
_____
_____

```
*  1)  more than one million two hundred
       thousand
   2)  more than three hundred thousand
   3)  more than fifty thousand
   4)  more than one hundred thousand
   5)  fewer than six hundred thousand
```

Subject Matter Review (continued)

2. _____
_____
_____
_____
_____

    1) WWI
    2) WWII
* 3) Korea
    4) Vietnam
    5) Korea and Vietnam combined

3. _____
_____
_____
_____
_____

    1) Korea
    2) WWI
* 3) WWII
    4) Vietnam
    5) WWI and Korea combined

4. _____
_____
_____
_____
_____

    1) WWI
    2) WWII
* 3) Korea
    4) Vietnam
    5) WWI total casualties minus dead and
       missing

Answers:
1. The total casualties of the U.S. in WWII were
2. In which war were the casualties the lowest?
3. There are many possible questions here. Some are:
    A. Which war had the greatest number of casualties?
    B. Which war had more casualties than all of the others combined?
    C. Which war had the most dead and missing?
    D. Which war was the only one to exceed 500,000 dead and missing?
4. Which war had the fewest casualties and the fewest dead and missing?

CHECK YOUR
ANSWERS

Now study this chart and do the same thing.

UNITED NATIONS CASUALTIES IN KOREAN WAR

PRACTICE
THE SKILLS

Country	Total Casualties	Dead	Wounded	Returned Missing	Prisoners
Australia	1,592	291	1,240	39	21
Belgium and Luxembourg	453	97	350	5	1
Canada	1,396	291	1,072	21	12
Colombia	686	140	452	65	29
Ethiopia	656	120	536	—	—
France	1,135	288	818	18	11
Greece	715	169	543	2	1
Netherlands	704	111	589	4	—
New Zealand	115	34	80	—	1
Philippines	488	92	299	57	40
Thailand	913	114	794	5	—
Turkey	3,349	717	2,246	167	219
Union of South Africa	42	20	—	16	6
United Kingdom	5,017	710	2,278	1,263	766
Totals	17,260	3,194	11,297	1,662	1,107
Republic of Korea	1,310,848	415,004	428,568	459,428	7,848
U.S.A.	157,530	54,246	103,284	760	5,133
Grand Total	1,485,638	472,444	543,149	461,850	14,088

1. _____
   _____
   _____
   _____
   _____

    1) Thailand
    2) Philippines
* 3) Union of South Africa
    4) Turkey
    5) Australia

2. _____
   _____
   _____
   _____
   _____

* 1) Republic of Korea
    2) Canada
    3) France
    4) Colombia
    5) Philippines

3. _____
   _____
   _____
   _____
   _____

```
  1)  fewer than WWI
  2)  fewer than Vietnam
  3)  more than the population of Vietnam
* 4)  more than WWII
  5)  more than all wars combined
```

Answers:
1. Which country had the fewest casualties?
2. Which country had the most casualties?
3. Which of the answers below *best* describes the total casualties of the Korean War?
If you didn't have these exact questions, you are not necessarily wrong. Have someone else check them out if you wonder about them.

**CHECK YOUR
ANSWERS**

The period covered in this program was a time of powerful people. Below is a list of some of them. Write the name of the country with which each was associated.

```
1. Mussolini    _____
2. Tojo         _____
3. Hitler       _____
4. Stalin       _____
5. Churchill    _____
6. Gen. Grove   _____
7. Oppenheimer  _____
8. Eisenhower   _____
```

**PRACTICE
THE SKILLS**

Answers:
1. Italy	2. Japan	3. Germany
4. Russia	5. England	6. U.S.A.
7. U.S.A.	8. U.S.A	

**CHECK YOUR
ANSWERS**

Just for Fun

Eleven years after the intricately planned and much publicized solo flight of Charles Lindbergh, Douglas Corrigan left New York in a ramshackle, over-loaded plane bound for California. Twenty-six hours later he landed in Ireland.

"I guess I just got lost in the fog," laughed Corrigan, who still lives in the record as "Wrong-Way Corrigan."

No one can say for sure whether Corrigan intended to fly the Atlantic, a flight for which special permission was needed, or was simply lost, as he claimed.

It is a curious fact that when Lindbergh took his plane, *The Spirit of St. Louis*, on its first test flight in San Diego, it was Corrigan who removed the blocks from the wheels. Did this close connection with an aviation great inspire Corrigan to cook up the greatest hoax in history?

Whether the incident was a case of poor navigation or a practical joke, it afforded a nation, still reeling from the Depression, something to smile about.

Test-Taking Tip

Your skill at analyzing maps, charts, and graphs is very important.

You can get a head start on questions about these materials if you understand the way ideas are organized in them. Below is a list of the major ways information is organized in maps and graphs.

1. *Time sequence.* Maps will often show how things looked in the past and how they look now. Graphs will frequently show how things were and either tell you or ask you to infer how the same items currently are.
2. *From general to specific.* This is especially true of charts and graphs. They will make a statement of the larger picture and compare it to specific ideas.
3. *From least to most or from most to least.* This also means smallest to largest, simple to complex, and so forth. Maps and charts are good devices to show *extremes.*
4. *Both sides of the story.* Pollsters are always making graphs telling how people respond to questions, whether pro or con.

Being able to recognize these elements when taking a test will increase your chances of scoring well.

Checklist

In order to give yourself a quick review of this chapter, compile the following information as you remember it from the workbook and the video.

PEOPLE	PLACES	DATES
_____	_____	_____
_____	_____	_____
_____	_____	_____
_____	_____	_____
_____	_____	_____
_____	_____	_____

Below is a crossword puzzle featuring words and concepts discussed in this learning series. Some of the words weren't used in the lessons, but you should be able to figure them out anyway.

PRACTICE THE SKILLS

Horizontal

1. in the time of
4. region at the top of the globe
9. osmium (symbol)
10. outside (Gr. prefix)
11. Gravity is great near a black one.
12. won the Civil War
15. modern wheel and axle
16. full of (L. suffix)
18. one who does (Gr. suffix)
20. ampere (abbrev.)
21. afternoon
22. mixture with large particles
23. against (L. prefix)
26. tellurium (symbol)
27. alone (L. prefix)
28. reason some people came to the New World
31. what gears do
33. center of cell and atom
36. compass point
37. relative acidity
38. cesium (symbol)
39. xenon (symbol)

Vertical

1. type of current caused by heat
2. same or equal (Gr. prefix)
3. genus: Felis
4. Germany and friends—WWII
5. determines genetic traits
6. digit
7. of (L. suffix)
8. smallest unit of life
13. radium (symbol)
14. our genus
17. United Press International
19. fish eggs
20. medicinal plant
24. body parts referred to by Greek prefix "osteo"
25. Pisces
28. aristocracy means rule by this
29. away from the wind
30. state of matter
32. six (L. prefix)
34. doesn't exist in space
35. not (L. prefix)

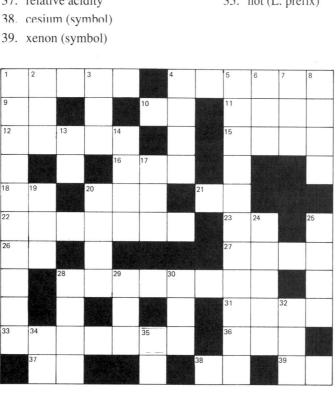

CHECK YOUR
ANSWERS

Chapter Sixteen
Social Studies

This is the last of the Social Studies lessons. In this lesson, we will once more apply all of those analysis skills we've been working on. This lesson will challenge your ability to keep the "actors" separated in your mind.

You will need to be "on your toes" while viewing this video. This was a time of diverse opinion, motives, and actions. Our country experienced much violence, turmoil, and strife, including the assassinations of three of our most important leaders. This negative side of our existence was balanced by some extreme heroism.

The program takes you to the beginnings, as much as possible, of the trends which affect us so greatly

today. To do this, the video must go back and forth in time. You will need to be alert to the time context of each segment.

The common denominator in all this is communication technology. First radio, and then television, made it possible for people all over the country to know of world events as they were happening.

This is the last lesson in this series. The major skills we will be dealing with are looking for the main idea when it's indirectly stated, sensing tone, determining viewpoint, and summarizing. If you still feel a little unsure about these skills, look back in the workbook to the pages where you practiced them before.

Vocabulary for Program 16

LEARN THE WORDS

Celluloid (SELL-you-loyd) is the trademarked name for a substance made from cellulose nitrate, used in the manufacture of film. It is used in this lesson to refer to motion pictures.

consumerism (kuhn-SOOM-uhr-iz-um) refers to activism supporting the interests of consumers.

credibility (kred-uh-BILL-it-ee) means "believability." During the era covered in this video, the presidency was said to "lack credibility."

assassin (uh-SASS-in) means someone who murders for hire or for political or religious motives.

escalate (ESS-kuh-late) means to increase gradually but steadily.

segregation (seg-ruh-GAY-shun) is the process of setting apart one group from another. It usually refers to separation of the races.

integration (in-tuh-GRAY-shun) means to put together into one unit. It's used here to mean the opposite of segregation.

discrimination (dis-crim-uh-NAY-shun) means making judgments about something or someone on the basis of a difference. It often refers to actions taken because of race. In this context, the word has a negative connotation.

feminist (FEM-uh-nist) is someone who works for the rights of women.

media (MEE-dee-uh) are substances on which something else is displayed, preserved, or transmitted. In this context, it refers to newspapers, radio, and television—which display and transmit information. Media is the plural of the word "medium" (MEE-dee-uhm).

domestic upheaval refers to societal unrest.

cult of personality, as it is used in this lesson, means the undue respect given to famous people. The word "cult" is used to indicate that this feeling of high regard is almost like a religion.

Silent Majority was the group of Americans who supposedly made up the major part of the population. This term was popular at the time of Richard Nixon, who viewed himself as the leader of this group.

WASP is a word made from the first letters of the words White Anglo-Saxon Protestant. It was used both as a term of contempt and as a slogan. A made-up word of this type is called an acronym (ACK-roh-nim).

Hawks and Doves. Hawks were people who thought that war and military action could solve the problems of the day. On the other side of the argument were the Doves, who sought solutions through peaceful means.

**Subject
Matter
Review**

**LEARN THE
FACTS**

1. From the end of WWII to the present, our country has undergone dramatic sociological changes.
2. Instant, worldwide communications have greatly influenced the way we think and behave.
3. Great strides have been made in the area of human rights. These domestic advances have been counterbalanced by continual global unrest and threats to peace.
4. Violence frequently had sickening outbreaks. Three of our most prominent leaders were assassinated.
5. The big issues of the period revolved around
   A. the Korean War
   B. the Cold War
   C. the Vietnam War
   D. race relations
   E. civil rights
   F. equal rights for women
   G. the energy crisis
   H. the space race
6. The Vietnam conflict was the longest and most unpopular war in our history.
7. Much of the negative reaction to the Vietnam War was caused by TV coverage, which brought the violence and destruction live into American homes.
8. Two famous "firsts" occurred during this period. Spaceflight started and the moon was explored. Also, we suffered through the first resignation of a president.

While 1960s American society was learning to communicate through the electronic media, the counter-cultures, of which there were many, were communicating and "relating to" some diverse folk media.

Buttons abounded. There was hardly a lapel that didn't sport at least one. Some people wore several in order to communicate their particular philosophies.

When buttons alone didn't quite tell the whole story, they were pinned on T-shirts, which were also printed with statements of opinion. The shirts' messages ran the spectrum from artful to vulgar, from deep to silly.

No hippie "pad" was considered complete unless the walls were covered with posters. This art form, called Pop Art, frequently incorporated the words of the aphorism into the design of the poster.

**PRACTICE
THE SKILLS**

Subject Matter Review (continued)

Perhaps no other communicationg art has shown as much imagination as the vigorous colors and words of the poster fad. From simple black and white statements to psychedelic phantasmagoria, these works of art changed the way we think about graphics.

When the tribe piled into their beat-up, hand-painted Volkswagen micro-bus, this peculiar form of communication continued. Stickers intended for bumpers spread like a creeping rash over the entire vehicle, including windows, imperiling any kind of reasonable vision.

Onlookers were faced with a constant dilemma, not knowing where the sincerity left off and the satire or outrageous leg-pulling began.

Now answer these questions.

1. In paragraph two, the word sport means   1. ① ② ③ ④ ⑤
    1) a game
    2) to wear
    3) a joke
    4) to play
    5) a gentleman

2. In paragraph four, the word pad means   2. ① ② ③ ④ ⑤
    1) apartment
    2) creep
    3) notebook
    4) cushion
    5) foot

3. Psychedelic phantasmagoria means   3. ① ② ③ ④ ⑤
    1) simple pictures
    2) wild, bright images
    3) politics
    4) hippies
    5) posters

4. Which is the best meaning for aphorism?   4. ① ② ③ ④ ⑤
    1) slogan
    2) sleep inducer
    3) love potion
    4) essay
    5) poster

Subject Matter Review (continued)

5. Choose the best title for this selection.   5. ① ② ③ ④ ⑤
   1) The Day of the Hippie
   2) Posters and Politics
   3) The Counter-Culture Communications
   4) Button Up for Protest
   5) Get Off My Back About My Shirt

Answers:
  1. 2   2. 1   3. 2   4. 1   5. 3

CHECK YOUR ANSWERS

PRACTICE THE SKILLS

The personal kinds of communication mentioned in the passage were supposed to tell how an individual felt or believed. Below are some examples of each of these media.

BUTTONS

Number 1

BLACK IS BEAUTIFUL

Number 2

SUPPORT OUR BOYS IN VIETNAM

Number 3

DON'T TRUST ANYONE OVER 30

Number 4

WE SHALL OVERCOME

Number 5

MY BUTTON LOVES YOUR BUTTON

Number 6

Legalize Spiritual Discovery

POSTERS

Number 7

Number 8

Number 9

Number 10

Number 11

Number 12

Subject Matter Review (continued)

T-SHIRTS

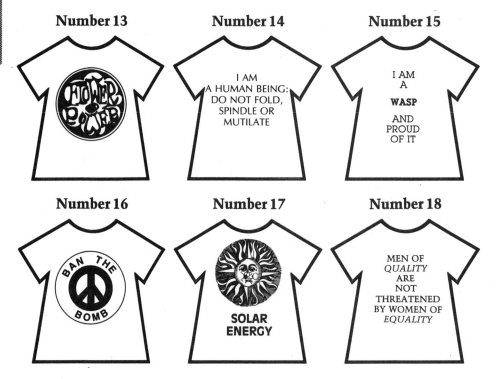

Number 13

Number 14
I AM
A HUMAN BEING:
DO NOT FOLD,
SPINDLE OR
MUTILATE

Number 15
I AM
A
WASP
AND
PROUD
OF IT

Number 16

Number 17
SOLAR
ENERGY

Number 18
MEN OF
QUALITY
ARE
NOT
THREATENED
BY WOMEN OF
EQUALITY

BUMPER STICKERS

Number 19

> **Hate the police? The next time you're in trouble, call a hippy.**

Number 20

> **3 G's that made America great:**
> **GOD GUNS GUTS**

Number 21

> **BUY A FOREIGN CAR**
> **Put 10 Americans out of work!**

Number 22

> **MAKE LOVE, NOT WAR**

Now answer these questions.

1. The button which is the most obvious example of "leg pulling" is
   1) No. 1
   2) No. 2
   3) No. 4
   4) No. 5
   5) No. 6

1. ① ② ③ ④ ⑤

2. In 1813, Admiral O.H. Perry sent a message to the president which said, "We have met the enemy and they are ours; two ships, two brigs, one schooner and one sloop." What is the number of the parody of this quote?
   1) No. 11
   2) No. 14
   3) No. 9
   4) No. 19
   5) No. 22

2. ① ② ③ ④ ⑤

3. President Carter called the energy crisis "the moral equivalent of war." What is the number of the message resulting from this statement?
   1) No. 2
   2) No. 7
   3) No. 10
   4) No. 14
   5) No. 19

3. ① ② ③ ④ ⑤

4. A black leader of this era said, "No one ever talked about 'white power' because power in this country is white." Which item refers to this statement?
   1) No. 1
   2) No. 5
   3) No. 13
   4) No. 4
   5) No. 21

4. ① ② ③ ④ ⑤

5. "LSD is Western yoga. The aim of all Eastern
religion, like the aim of LSD, is basically
to get high; that is, to expand your con-
sciousness and find ecstasy and revelation
within." This quote from Dr. Timothy Leary
refers to which of the numbered items above?
1) No. 4
2) No. 6
3) No. 11
4) No. 15
5) No. 20

5. ① ② ③ ④ ⑤

6. Poster number 7 implies
1) Schools have all the money they need.
2) The Air Force is going to start having
bake sales.
3) Children are "on top of the world."
4) Ban the bomb.
5) We are putting the emphasis in the wrong
place.

6. ① ② ③ ④ ⑤

7. Bob Hope said, "If we ever let the Communists
win this war, we are in danger of fighting
for the rest of our lives and losing a million kids." According to this statement,
which button would Bob Hope most likely wear?
1) No. 6
2) No. 5
3) No. 3
4) No. 2
5) No. 1

7. ① ② ③ ④ ⑤

8. Which of the numbered items is a protest
against the computer age?
1) No. 5
2) No. 10
3) No. 11
4) No. 12
5) No. 14

8. ① ② ③ ④ ⑤

9. Martin Luther King, Jr. said, "I have a dream
   that my four little children will one day
   live in a nation where they will not be
   judged by the color of their skin but by the
   content of their character." Which button
   would Martin Luther King, Jr. have worn?
   1) No. 2
   2) No. 6
   3) No. 3
   4) No. 4
   5) No. 5

9. ① ② ③ ④ ⑤

10. If you were concerned about the environment
    and all the pollutants our society puts into
    the air and water, which of these posters
    would you like best?
    1) No. 8
    2) No. 9
    3) No. 10
    4) No. 11
    5) No. 12

10. ① ② ③ ④ ⑤

11. Here is an excerpt from "Alice's Restaurant"
    by Arlo Guthrie.

    **"And I walked in, I sat down, they gave me a piece of paper
    that said, 'Kid, see the psychiatrist, room 604.' I went in and I
    said, 'Shrink, I wanna kill. I wanna kill! I wanna see blood
    and gore and guts and veins in my teeth! Eat dead bodies,
    burnt bodies: I mean, kill!' And I started jumpin' up and
    down, yellin', 'Kill! Kill!' and he started jumpin' up and
    down yellin', 'Kill! Kill!' and the sergeant came over and
    pinned a medal on me."**

    Assuming this recruiting office scene is
    satire, which one of the following would Arlo
    Guthrie approve of least?
    1) No. 16
    2) No. 22
    3) No. 10
    4) No. 2
    5) No. 7

11. ① ② ③ ④ ⑤

Subject
Matter
Review
(continued)

12. Media expert Marshall McLuhan said, "Time has
    ceased, space has vanished. We now live in a
    global village … a simultaneous happening."
    Which of the following goes against this
    concept?
    1) No. 21
    2) No. 15
    3) No. 14
    4) No. 6
    5) No. 5

12. ① ② ③ ④ ⑤

Answers:

1. 5	2. 3	3. 4	4. 1
5. 2	6. 5	7. 4	8. 5
9. 4	10. 2	11. 4	12. 1

CHECK YOUR
ANSWERS

Just for Fun

People were always doing their "own things" during this period of time. Now you have a chance to do it. In the space below, design the button, T-shirt, and bumper sticker that really express your philosophy. This isn't as easy as it sounds. You can't use many words, so you have to choose them carefully.

My button would say: _____

My poster would say: _____

My T-shirt would say: _____

My bumper sticker would say: _____

Test-Taking Tip

When you're asked to evaluate information similar to the material covered in this chapter, think about cause and effect. The button "Black Is Beautiful" has no meaning unless you know a little about what caused people to wear it and what effect it had on others.

If all else fails, you can always fall back on the three evaluation questions: "What is it?" "What's it about?" "How do I know?"

Subject Matter Review (continued)

Checklist

To check your progress, go back to the beginning of the chapter and review all the activities in the book and the video. In the space below, compile a list of the most important events of the time.

Arrange them according to sequence and show how cause and effect are related. Also compile a list of the major ideas of the time.

EVENTS (in sequence)

1. _____

2. _____

3. _____

4. _____

5. _____

6. _____

7. _____

8. _____

9. _____

10. _____

CAUSE AND EFFECT

_____ caused _____

_____ caused _____

_____ caused _____

_____ caused _____

_____ caused _____

Subject Matter Review (continued)

IMPORTANT IDEAS AND CONCEPTS

1. _____

2. _____

3. _____

4. _____

5. _____

EXTRA-PRACTICE

We've been giving you Test-Taking Tips in every chapter. Here is a compiled list of the best suggestions from many sources.

I.   Listen carefully to all the directions given by the tester.

It might seem this suggestion would go without saying. However, people who give tests report that many errors are made because of inattention. Listen intently to the tester's instructions and follow them exactly.

II.   Budget your time wisely.

We've hinted at this all along. Remember some of the techniques we've talked about that will help you.

III.   Survey the whole test section before answering any questions. Read all the questions carefully.

Use your scanning skills.

IV.   Do the easy questions first.

How many times have we said this? Zipping through the easy questions gives you more time to work on the hard ones. You also buy time to figure out some of the items that take more complex reasoning.

Transferring answers to the answer sheet takes time, too. Before you take the test, review the section on filling out the answer sheet.

V.   Read, read, and re-read.

You've got to read the "information input," which may be a story, article, map, chart, graph, or illustration. Then you must record your answer correctly.

If there's a question you've left out and need to go back to answer, try reading the question before you re-read the selection. Guess only when you have to.

Subject Matter Review (continued)

VI.   When you have to guess, do it intelligently.

Here is a "guessing" strategy that might help you.

A.   Use the process of elimination.

1.   Eliminate the obviously wrong.

2.   Eliminate, for a time at least, those answers you think are partly wrong.

3.   Sometimes answers are correct statements of fact but do not have anything to do with the response asked for. Be careful here.

4.   Often you will find two responses that are exact opposites. More often than not one of these "twins" is the correct answer. You can probably ignore the other responses and concentrate on which one of the two is the right answer to the question.

B.   Choose the answer that is parallel to the question. Look for grammar clues.

C.   Failing all of the above, close your eyes and pick one. Answer every question—even if you have to guess.

VII.   Put the question into your own words (paraphrase).

This is where your ability in the use of context clues makes a big difference. Don't let unfamiliar words slow you down.

VIII. Information from one question may be helpful in answering another.

Think of the test as another learning situation. Any idea you can pick up during the test is just that much more knowledge. Remember, you can only learn more. You can't learn less.

IX.   Don't agonize. Trust your instincts.

Common sense will take you a long way in any test. If you've worked through this KET learning program faithfully, you have gained lots of new information. You have done well on one study exercise after another. Be confident and calm.

X.   Be a good editor.

Saving time at the beginning of the test allows you to carefully check your answers toward the end of the test session. Some people say, "I never change an answer." When they say that, you know they aren't very test-wise, because "never" is one of those qualifying words used in tests that tends to make for an incorrect response.

XI.   Never give up.

Make them chase you out of the testing room. Example:

Which of the following people gave up when the going got tough?
1. George Washington
2. Thomas Jefferson
3. Abraham Lincoln
4. Z. Walker Jennings

'Nuff said?

Post-Test

DIRECTIONS: Complete the following exercises and check your results. Review the sections of the workbook indicated by the Prescription for Further Study.

Questions 1 to 7 refer to the following passage.

Poverty is wonderful! Ask any married couple when the "good times" were, and they will almost always recount the days when they were poor, struggling youngsters fighting together just to scrape by. They tell you that now. They wouldn't have said the same thing then.

There was the agony, the uncertainty, but we remember the simple pleasures as if they were grand occasions. We celebrated minor events and toasted the splendor of the evening with wine we bought with our last ninety cents. Its bouquet lingers still as if it had been the finest imported Chablis.

Oh, to have the joys of poverty and the convenience of wealth!

1. The author gets your attention right away by   1.① ② ③ ④ ⑤
   1) using a startling statement
   2) stating an absolute truth
   3) telling how to prove his point
   4) implying that poverty is inconvenient
   5) using a cause-and-effect relationship

2. Which of the following expressions is the best description of what the passage is about?   2. ① ② ③ ④ ⑤
   1) A penny saved is a penny earned.
   2) You never miss the water 'til the well runs dry.
   3) It's not how much you have but how much you enjoy that makes happiness.
   4) The longest decade occurs between the ages of 10 and 20. They get increasingly shorter after that.
   5) Smile and the world smiles with you; cry and you cry alone.

3. Which of the following would be the best substitute for the last sentence of this passage?   3. ① ② ③ ④ ⑤
   1) So if you want to be happy, be poor.
   2) It's more fun to think about being poor if you are rich.
   3) So you see, you can be poor and rich at the same time.
   4) The rich can never know what happiness really is.
   5) This is the reason rich people should start out poor.

4. "Nostalgia" means sentimental yearning for the past. Which of the following lines from the passage is the most nostalgic?   4. ① ② ③ ④ ⑤
   1) Poverty is wonderful.
   2) There was the agony …
   3) They wouldn't have said the same thing then.
   4) Its bouquet lingers still as if it were the finest imported Chablis.
   5) Ask any married couple when the good times were …

5. This passage would mean the most to   5. ① ② ③ ④ ⑤
   1) people who have always been poor
   2) people who were poor but no longer are
   3) people who have always been rich
   4) children who live in poverty
   5) children from rich families

6. The passage implies that   6.① ② ③ ④ ⑤
   1) poverty really is wonderful
   2) only the poor can enjoy the splendor of
      an evening
   3) when we look back on hard times, we for-
      get the pain
   4) it's OK to be poor
   5) cheap wine is just as good as expensive
      wine

7. You can infer from this passage that   7.① ② ③ ④ ⑤
   1) the author was never poor
   2) things are never as good nor as bad as
      they seem
   3) our society makes too much of the evils
      of poverty
   4) poor people have an advantage over rich
      people
   5) all rich people secretly wish they were
      poor

Questions 8 to 11 refer to the following passage.

Foods we eat tend to spoil unless they are treated by one of many preservative techniques. The most popular techniques employed currently are canning and freezing. These processes destroy the bacteria which cause spoilage in the food—and cause disease in humans.

Some preservation practices date back into antiquity. Drying, salting or curing, and treating food with herbs and spices are practices that have been used since prehistoric times. Wines and vinegars were popular as preservatives in the days of the Bible. "Larding," a technique used by American pioneers, involved submerging pre-cooked meat in its own fat and storing it in crocks. The "lard" kept the bacteria-laden air away from the meat.

Newer methods include irradiation, exposing the food to a source of radiation, which keeps certain food from spoiling for many years.

8. Which of the following is the correct time   8.① ② ③ ④ ⑤
   sequence for the use of preservation techniques (earliest to latest)?
   1) canning, spices, drying, irradiation
   2) vinegars, spices, drying, canning
   3) curing, wines, larding
   4) larding, curing, drying, herbs
   5) herbs, irradiation, vinegars

9. What does the word "antiquity" mean as it is   9. ① ② ③ ④ ⑤
used in the passage?
   1) fairly old
   2) recent
   3) ancient times
   4) calendars
   5) preservation techniques

10. What is the major cause of food spoilage   10. ① ② ③ ④ ⑤
listed in the passage?
   1) pre-cooking
   2) air
   3) lard
   4) lack of adequate preservation practices
   5) bacteria

11. Which of the following is the best title for   11. ① ② ③ ④ ⑤
this passage?
   1) All About Food Preservation
   2) Food Preservation Long Ago
   3) A Short History of Food Preservation
      Practices
   4) How To Protect Your Food
   5) Prevention of Disease

Questions 12 to 16 refer to this passage.

John Bartram, a middle-aged, illiterate farmer in Colonial America, looked closely at a flower for the first time and so decided to devote the rest of his life to science.

According to the legend, he went to Philadelphia, the cultural center of the colonies, and bought a science book, which was written in Latin, and an English-Latin dictionary and learned to read both. He went on to collect specimens of plants, which he sent to the greats of science in Europe, including Linnaeus, the father of biology, who said that Bartram was the best natural botanist in the world.

It is said that Bartram died of fright as the British army approached Philadelphia, for he feared the army would destroy his arboretum.

A little over a hundred years later, Charles Deam, a highly trained pharmacist and self-taught botanist, distinguished himself by identifying and classifying thousands of the woodland plants of the Midwest.

Ironically, both of these two men share another distinction. They each discovered a tree which was the only one of its kind ever seen in the wild. Bartram named his the Ben Franklin tree after his friend and benefactor. The Deam Oak still stands serenely along a secondary highway near Bluffton, Indiana, where Deam saved this "one of a kind" from the woodsman's axe.

12. Which of the following tells the major way Deam and Bartram were alike? They both
    1) were uneducated
    2) lived in Colonial times
    3) feared the British
    4) learned about botany on their own
    5) were druggists

12. ① ② ③ ④ ⑤

13. Which of the following approximates the time during which Charles Deam lived?
    1) late 1700s
    2) early 1800s
    3) late 1800s
    4) late 1900s
    5) There isn't enough information given in the passage to know.

13. ① ② ③ ④ ⑤

14. The passage tells
    1) where to find the Ben Franklin tree
    2) where to find the Deam Oak
    3) how many specimens were identified by these scientists
    4) why they decided to become scientists
    5) why both men became important historical figures

14. ① ② ③ ④ ⑤

15. The passage implies
    1) botany is a science that can easily be learned
    2) the men were unusual because they taught themselves the science of botany
    3) it's easy for self-taught botanists to find a tree that no one else ever has
    4) illiterate means the same as unintelligent
    5) Deam was a better scientist than Bartram

15. ① ② ③ ④ ⑤

16. What does "ironically" mean as it's used in this passage?
    1) strangely
    2) not surprisingly
    3) unfortunately
    4) by the way
    5) supposedly

16. ① ② ③ ④ ⑤

CHALLENGE QUESTIONS (Optional)

A distraught man came to Socrates. The man had tried to build a temple, but it resembled a mud hut and not the Parthenon. Socrates said to the man:

Take heart for there are few enough men who would build a Parthenon, but of the few, for the most part build themselves a mud hut and call it a Parthenon.

And the man went home and built his temple.

17. The man was upset because
    1) Socrates was unsympathetic
    2) he had built a mud hut
    3) he felt as if he had failed
    4) a Parthenon was too difficult to build
    5) someone else had already built a Parthenon

17. ① ② ③ ④ ⑤

18. Which of the following best tells what Socrates told the man?
    1) You are a failure because you can only build mud huts.
    2) Continue to build mud huts and let other people build the temples.
    3) You are more honest than most people because you see your creation for what it is.
    4) Most people create one thing and tell you it's something else.
    5) both 3) and 4)

18. ① ② ③ ④ ⑤

Answers for Post-Test:

1. 1	2. 3	3. 2	4. 4	5. 2
6. 3	7. 2	8. 3	9. 3	10. 5
11. 3	12. 4	13. 3	14. 2	15. 2
16. 1	17. 3	18. 5		

CHECK YOUR ANSWERS

Prescription for Further Study

On question	if you answered	you were wrong because	you should review
1.	2)	there are few absolutes	Test-Taking Tip (16)
	3)	this isn't an attention-getting device	style (4 and 9)
	4)	this asks about motive	motive (3)
2.	1)	this is not the main idea	main idea (2)
	2)	this is the opposite of the implied idea	main idea (2 and 3)
	4)	this is irrelevant	main idea (2 and 3)
3.	1)	the passage doesn't say this	main idea (1, 2, and 3)
	3)	it doesn't make any sense	inference (2 and 4)
	5)	it could be right but it's weak	Test-Taking Tip (all)
4.	1)	this is not nostalgic	satire (2 and 3)
	2), 3), or 5)	this is supporting detail	detail (2, 3, and 4)
5.	1), 3), 4), or 5)	none of these has the proper point of view	point of view (1 and 8)
6.	1)	this is faulty inference	inference (2, 3, and 4)
	2)	this is the wrong detail	detail (2, 3, and 4)
	4)	this isn't implied	inference (4)
	5)	this is a faulty inference	inference (1, 2, and 3)

Prescription for Further Study (continued)

On question	if you answered	you were wrong because	you should review
7.	1)	the author uses "we"	motive (3)
	3)	the passage doesn't suggest this	detail (2)
	4)	not as strong an answer	inference (3)
	5)	"all" tells you to avoid this choice	Test-Taking Tip (14)
8.	1), 2), 4), or 5)	the sequence is a supporting detail in this question	sequence (2)
9.	1), 2), 4),	only "ancient times" fits the context	context (1, 2, and 8)
10.	1), 2), 3),	the details don't fit the question	detail (8, 9, and 10)
11.	1)	the article doesn't tell everything about preservation	main idea (9)
	2)	it's also about current practices	main idea (1 and 10)
	4)	it's a weak answer	main idea (1, 2, and 7)
	5)	this is just a detail	detail (1 and 6)
12.	1)	only Bartram was uneducated	comparison (1)
	2)	only Bartram lived in colonial times	detail (1)
	3)	only Bartram feared the British	comparison (1)
	5)	only Deam was a druggist	detail (1 and 2)

On question	if you answered	you were wrong because	you should review
13.	1)	only Bartram lived in the 1700s	detail (12)
	2)	early 1800s is not 100 years after the late 1700s	synthesis (13 and 15)
	4)	late 1900s is more than 100 years after late 1700s	synthesis (13 and 15)
	5)	it does tell indirectly when Deam lived	sequence (1)
14.	1)	it doesn't tell	detail (15)
	3)	this isn't mentioned	detail (8 and 15)
	4)	it doesn't tell "why"	motive (3 and 7)
	5)	neither is famous in history	(12)
15.	1)	the passage suggests botany is not easily learned	tone (8 and 9)
	3)	this isn't implied	irrelevance (2 and 8)
	4)	this isn't implied	detail (13)
	5)	no such comparison is made	comparison (14 and 15)
16.	2)	this is the opposite of what the passage says	Test-Taking Tips
	3)	this isn't implied	context (16)
	4)	this has the wrong emphasis	emphasis (3 and 7)
	5)	this is out of context	context (14, 15, and 16)

**Prescription
for
Further
Study**
(continued)

On question	if you answered	you were wrong because	you should review
17.	1)	this is the opposite of what is said	Test-Taking Tips
	2)	he had wanted to build something else	main idea (13 and 14)
	4)	it's irrelevant	(8)
	5)	it's irrelevant	(8)
18.	1)	this is the opposite of what he said	main idea (2, 12, and 16)
	2)	Socrates didn't say this	main idea (3, 12, and 16)
	3) or 4)	each of these answers is right BUT ... it's more complete when 3) and 4) are combined	synthesis (12, 13, and 16)

Acknowledgements

CHAPTER ONE

Excerpt reprinted by permission of Grosset & Dunlap from NATIVE TONGUES by Charles Berlitz, copyright 1982 by Charles Berlitz.

CHAPTER TWO

"There Is No Frigate LIke a Book" by Emily Dickinson. Reprinted by permission of the publishers and the Trustees of Amherst College. From THE POEMS OF EMILY DICKINSON, edited by Thomas H. Johnson, Cambridge, Mass.; The Belknap Press of Harvard University Press, copyright 1951, 1955, 1979, 1983 by The President and Fellows of Harvard College.
"Stopping by Woods on a Snowy Evening" from THE POETRY OF ROBERT FROST, edited by Edward Connery Lathem. Copyright 1923, 1969 by Holt, Rinehart and Winston. Copyright 1951 by Robert Frost. Reprinted by permission of Holt, Rinehart and Winston, publishers.
"Richard Cory" from THE CHILDREN OF THE NIGHT by Edwin Arlington Robinson. Published by Charles Scribner's Sons, New York.
Excerpt from "the lives and times of archy and mehitable" by Don Marquis. Copyright 1927, 1930, 1933 by Doubleday & Company, Inc. Reprinted by permission of the publisher.
Excerpt from THE PETRIFIED MAN copyright 1939, 1967 by Eudora Welty. Reprinted from her volume A CURTAIN OF GREEN AND OTHER STORIES by permission of Harcourt Brace Javanovich, Inc.

CHAPTER THREE

"when my canary ... " from CRICKET SONGS, Japanese haiku translated by Harry Behn. Copyright 1964 by Harry Behn. All rights reserved. Reprinted by permission of Marian Reiner.
"you can't ask a man ..." from RAINWATER CHRONICLES copyright 1982 Jefferson Danyal. Reprinted with permission.

CHARPTER FOUR

Excerpts from THE GLASS MENAGERIE by Tennessee Williams. Copyright 1945 by Tennessee Williams and Edwina D. Williams and renewed 1973 by Tennessee Williams. Reprinted by permission of Random House, Inc.

CHAPTER FIVE

Burr Shafer cartoon reprinted from THE WONDERFUL WORLD OF J. WESLEY SMITH by Burr Shafer by persmission of the publisher, Vanguard Press, Inc. Copyright 1960 by Burr Shafer.
Sheet music cartoon from THE BEST OF RUBE GOLDBERG by Charles Keller; copyright 1979 by Rube Goldberg. Reprinted by permission of the publisher.
Dana Summers cartoon from THE ORLANDO SENTINEL.
Elevator cartoon from LADIES AND GENTLEMEN by Peter Arno. Copyright 1955 by Peter Arno; copyright 1983 by Patricia Arno. Reprinted by permission of Simon & Schuster, Inc.

CHAPTER SIX

Excerpt from "Seven Wonder" in LATE NIGHT THOUGHTS ON LISTENING TO MAHLER'S NINTH SYMPHONY by Lewis Thomas. Copyright 1983 by Lewis Thomas. Reprinted by permission of Viking Penguin Inc.

CHAPTER ELEVEN

Answer sheet for GED test reprinted by permission of The General Educational Development Testing Service.

CHAPTER THIRTEEN

"Cherokees Let State Keep Sacred Land" reprinted by permission of United Press International, Inc.

CHAPTER FOURTEEN

Cartoon, "Progress," from LIFE, 1915. Reprinted by permission of Rockwell, DeWitt, Conklin Organization.

CHAPTER SIXTEEN

Poster reprinted by permission of the Women's International League for Peace and Freedom, Philadelphia, PA.

Credits

SCIENCE SERIES CREDITS

Pamela Lewis
Series Host

Casting Consultation by:
Theatre Communications Group,
New York

Charles Barnett
Los Alamos National Laboratory
Los Alamos, New Mexico

California Academy of Sciences
San Francisco, California

John Corso
W.A. Palmer Studios
Belmont, California

Billie Deason
Johnson Space Center
Houston, Texas

Sylvia Earle
California Academy of Sciences
San Francisco, California

Tony Ellington
NASA
Washington, D.C.

James M. GAVER
U.S. Department of Energy
Aiken, South Carolina

Greg Gerlock
WLEX-TV, Channel 18
Lexington, Kentucky

Sheldon Glashow
Harvard University
Cambridge, Massachusetts

Robert and Lynne Goldsmith
Lexington, Kentucky

Harvard University
Cambridge, Massachusetts

Harry Hertzer
NASA
Washington, D.C.

U.S. Representative Larry
Hopkins
Kentucky

Mike Howard
Fayette County Schools
Lexington, Kentucky

Jennifer Jacobs
Lexington, Kentucky

Kimberly Jacobs
Lexington, Kentucky

Dale F. Keller Jr.
Defense Nuclear Agency
Alexandria, Virginia

Buford Knowles
U.S. Postal Service
Washington, D.C.

Dave Landers
WKYT-TV, Channel 27
Lexington, Kentucky

William McGorry
Young and Rubicam
New York, New York

Massachusetts Institute of
Technology
Cambridge, Massachusetts

Judith Mattingly
Lexington, Kentucky

Metropolitan Dade County
Department of Tourism
Miami, Florida

Philip Morrison
MIT
Cambridge, Massachusetts

Story Musgrave
Johnson Space Center
Houston, Texas

Sharon O'Brien
National Geographic Society
Washington, D.C.

Mrs. Tracy Randall
Lexington, Kentucky

Sally Ride
Johnson Space Center
Houston, Texas

Kathryn Sullivan
Johnson Space Center
Houston, Texas

Bill Tobey
Harvard University
Cambridge, Massachusetts

Mrs. Le Thu Tran
Nicholasville, Kentucky

Wilco Travel Agency
Lexington, Kentucky

Pam Wing
California Academy of Sciences
San Francisco, California

SOCIAL STUDIES SERIES
CREDITS

Wayne Bryan
Series Host

Players:
Baxter Harris
Laura Hicks
Debroah Mayo
Julie Rodgers
Joan Shangold
Christie Tate
William Van Hunter

Casting Consultation by
Theatre Communications Group,
New York

American Antiquarian Society

Brown Brothers

Chicago Historical Society

Courier-Journal & Louisville
Times

Culver Pictures, Inc.

Defense Audio Visual Agency

Eugene C. Barker Texas History
Center

Ford Motor Company

Historical Society of
Pennsylvania

Illinois State Historical Library

L. Michael Lewis

Library of Congress

Los Alamos National Laboratory

Martin Luther King Public
Library

Metropolitan Museum of Art

Museum of the City of New York

NAACP

National Archives Motion Picture
Branch

National Archives Still Picture
Branch

National Museum of American
History, Smithsonian Institution

New York Historical Society

New York Public Library

Nixon Project

Office of the Architect of the
Capitol

Tennessee Valley Authority

Veterans Administration

Washington Post

Winterthur Museum

Woolaroc Museum

Motion Picture Research
David Thaxton
Kevin Green

Still Picture Research
Linda Christenson
Doris Geoghegen

PRODUCTION CREDITS

Reading Skills

Sid Webb
Executive Producer

Guy Mendes
Judy Tipton
Writers

David Ray Robinson
Bob Simmons
Camera

Mike Heaton
Lighting Director

Terry Schoen
Film

Gary Mosley
Roger Tremaine
Walter Scott
Audio

Judy Tipton
Producer

Catherine Henschen
Luralyn Lahr
Associate Producers

Joy Flynn
Floor Director

Missy Holloway
Fred Rivers
Sets

Walter Houghton
Hank Batts
Video

Heather McAdams
Portraits

Russ Farmer
Guy Mendes
Directors

Martha Chute
Aurora Graphics Coordinator

Jo Motsinger
Costumes and Makeup

Otis Ballard
James Walker
Videotape Editors

Tom Fitzpatrick
Bob Hutchison
Jamie Urquhart
Videotape

Tamara Webb
Electronic Graphics

Science

Sid Webb
Executive Producer

Catherine Henschen
Associate Producer

Ed Shuman
Floor Director

Jim Bugay
David Ray Robinson
Cameras

Tamara Webb
Electronic Graphics

Gail Worth
Film

Judy Tipton
Producer

Richard Smith
Writer

Mike Heaton
Lighting Director

Calvin Smith
Audio

Tom Fitzpatrick
Fran Hardaway
Videotape

Russ Farmer
Director

Martha Chute
Aurora Graphics Coordinator

Jo Motsinger
Costumes and Makeup

Walter Houghton
Video

James Walker
Videotape Editor

Chela Kaplan
David Crawford
Still Photography

Social Studies

Sid Webb
Executive Producer

Luralyn Lahr
Associate Producer

Judy Tipton
Producer

Guy Mendes
Writer

Vince Spoelker
Director

Mike Heaton
Edward Shuman
Lighting Directors

Edward Shuman
Charlee Heaton
Floor Directors

Bob Hutchinson
James Walker
Viedotape

Fred Rivers
Sets

David Thaxton
Kevin Green
Motion Picture Research

Bob Simmons
David Ray Robinson
Joy Flynn
Carl Jarecky
Cameras

Gary Mosley
Calvin Smith
Audio

Martha Chute
Aurora Graphics Coordinator

Linda Christenson
Doris Geoghegen
Still Picture Research

Walter Houghton
Video

James Walker
Videotape Editor

Jo Motsinger
Kay Sternberg
Costumes and Makeup

Tamara Webb
Electronic Graphics

National Advisory Committee Members, 1984-1985

Bob Allen	Texas Education Agency
Douglas Bodwell	Corporation for Public Broadcasting
William Box	Mississippi Department of Education
Lila Camburn	Pascagoula (MS) School District
Dr. Robert Clausen	Oregon Department of Education
Jean Coleman	American Library Association
Sharon Darling	Kentucky Department of Education
Samuel Delaney	Fayette Co. (KY) Board of Education
Paul Delker	U.S. Department of Education
Luke Easter	Tennessee Department of Education
Dr. Robert Emmitt	U.S. Department of Labor
Dr. Gary Eyre	Council on Education
George Eyster	Morehead State University
Joan Flanery	Ashland (KY) Adult Ed. Learning Center
Dr. James Fouche	Kentucky Department of Education
Virginia Fox	Southern Educational Communications Association
Alan Garinger	Author
Chuck Guthrie	Murray State University
Tom Hale	Jefferson County (KY) Public Schools
Dr. John Hartwig	Iowa Department of Public Instruction
Beverly Herrlinger	Louisville (KY) Adult Ed. Learning Center
Lawrence Holden	Mississippi Educational Television
Paris Hopkins	Kentucky Office of Vocational Rehabilitation
Nancy Husk	Louisville (KY) Adult Ed. Learning Center
Sharon Jackson	Morehead State University
John Keenan	University of Maryland
Gentry LaRue	Fayette Co. (KY) Public Schools
Christie Maloney	University of Louisville
Charlotte Martin	Wisconsin Board of Voc-Tech-Ad Education
Sylvia McCollum	Federal Bureau of Prisons
Garrett Murphy	New York State Education Department
James Nelson	Kentucky Department of Libraries
Diane Owens	DANTES
Wayne Patience	American Council on Education
Virginia Portlock	Chicago City Colleges
Wilburn Pratt	Kentucky Office of Vocational Education
Constance Queen	Mississippi Educational Television
Barry Semple	New Jersey Department of Education
Buell Snyder	Jefferson Co. (KY) Public Schools
Mary Williams	Indiana Division of Adult Education
Jerry Wilson	Kentucky Dept. of Adult Correctional Institutions